CROSS-TRAINING FOR SPORTS

Gary T. Moran, PhD

George H. McGlynn, EdD
University of San Francisco

Human Kinetics

Library of Congress Cataloging-in-Publication Data

Moran, Gary T., 1994-
    Cross-training for sports / Gary T. Moran, George H. McGlynn.
      p.   cm.
    ISBN 0-88011-493-2
    1. Physical education and training. 2. Exercise. 3. Physical
fitness. I. McGlynn, George. II. Title
GV711.5.M67 1967
613.7'11--dc21

ISBN: 0-88011-493-2

96-52228
CIP

Copyright © 1997 by Gary T. Moran and George H. McGlynn

Table 2.1 on page 11 is reprinted from "1.5 mile tests," *The Aerobics Program for Total Well Being* By Kenneth H. Cooper, M.P.H. Copyright © 1982 by Kenneth H. Cooper. Used by permission of Bantam Books, a division of Bantam Doubleday Dell Publishing Group, Inc.

Figure 2.2 on page 15 is reprinted from *Aerobic Weight Training* by Frederick C. Hatfield © 1985. Used with permission of Contemporary Books, Inc., Chicago.

Figure 2.3 on page 16 is reprinted, by permission, from G. Borg, 1985, *An Introduction to Borg's RPE-scale* (Ithaca, N.Y.: Mouvement Publications).

Table 3.1 on page 32 is reprinted, by permission, from D. Wathen and F. Roll, 1994, "Training Methods and Modes" in *Essentials of Strength Training and Conditioning,* edited by T.R. Baechle (Champaign, IL: Human Kinetics Publishers), 404.

Table 3.2 on page 34 is reprinted, by permission, from D. Wathen, 1994, "Periodization: Concepts and Applications" in *Essentials of Strength Training and Conditioning,* edited by T.R. Baechle (Champaign, IL: Human Kinetics Publishers), 465-466.

Table 3.3 on page 41 is reprinted, by permission, from W.B. Allerheiligen, 1994, "Speed Development and Plyometric Training" in *Essentials of Strength Training and Conditioning,* edited by T.R. Baechle (Champaign, IL: Human Kinetics Publishers), 325.

Developmental Editor: Kirby Mittelmeier; **Assistant Editor:** Jennifer Stallard; **Editorial Assistants:** Amy Carnes, Jennifer Hemphill; **Copyeditor:** Amie Bell; **Proofreader:** Debra Aglaia; **Graphic Designer:** Stuart Cartwright; **Graphic Artist:** Angela Snyder; **Photo Editor:** Boyd LaFoon; **Cover Designer:** Jack Davis; **Photographer (cover):** Anthony Neste; **Illustrator:** Richard Schmidt; **Printer:** Versa Press

Human Kinetics books are available at special discounts for bulk purchase. Special editions or book excerpts can also be created to specification. For details, contact the Special Sales Manager at Human Kinetics.

Printed in the United States of America

10 9 8 7 6 5 4 3 2 1

Human Kinetics
Web site: http://www.humankinetics.com/

United States: Human Kinetics
P.O. Box 5076
Champaign, IL 61825-5076
1-800-747-4457
e-mail: humank@hkusa.com

Canada: Human Kinetics, Box 24040
Windsor, ON N8Y 4Y9
1-800-465-7301 (in Canada only)
e-mail: humank@hkeurope.com

Europe: Human Kinetics, P.O. Box IW14
Leeds LS16 6TR, United Kingdom
(44) 1132 781708
e-mail: humank@hkeurope.com

Australia: Human Kinetics
57A Price Avenue
Lower Mitcham, South Australia 5062
(08) 277 1555
e-mail: humank@hkaustralia.com

New Zealand: Human Kinetics
P.O. Box 105-231, Auckland 1
(09) 523 3462
e-mail: humank@hknewz.com

To my wife, Jodie Susan Moran, for your friendship, loyalty, and love, and in memory of Tuffy, male boxer, my training partner for many years and many miles
  —Gary T. Moran

To my wife, Ingeborg, and son, George
  —George H. McGlynn

Contents

Preface

In the early 1990s, the number of athletes using cross-training to help them improve their primary-sport performance and maintain all-around conditioning is booming. Cross-training for many has become a byword for training. Over the last few years a myriad of new cross-training activities, techniques, and devices have been introduced, making it extremely difficult for the average athlete to distinguish between what is valid and safe and what is ineffectual or even dangerous.

The purpose of this book is to bridge the gap between scientific knowledge and useful application by providing athletes and coaches the most efficient and up-to-date methods of cross-training to ensure that their training programs are beneficial and safe.

The text covers all the important aspects of cross-training. Part I is divided into five chapters that cover training for the major fitness components of aerobic and anaerobic endurance; muscle strength, power, and endurance; and agility, balance, and flexibility. Chapter 1 begins by providing some background about the history of cross-training and the type of physiological and psychological benefits it produces. Chapters 2-4 explain fitness principles and guidelines. Chapter 5 synthesizes this knowledge and shows you how to integrate cross-training into training for your primary sport.

The chapters in part II detail sport-specific cross-training options for 26 different sports. The sport-specific chapters are grouped under five major categories that reflect the unique demands of each activity: aerobic sports, sprinting sports, power sports, throwing and striking sports, and multisports. Each chapter begins with a brief analysis of the important aspects of cross-training specific to the sport, then provides an easy-to-read matrix that matches fitness components, such as warm-up and cool-down, aerobic and anaerobic training, muscle endurance and strength, and flexibility, with a variety of compatible and beneficial cross-training methods and activities.

Also included are three-, five-, and seven-day aerobic/anaerobic exercise example programs, plus the most effective weight training and flexibility exercises for each sport. Illustrations and exercise descriptions are provided to help readers understand and properly execute the recommended exercises.

The information in *Cross-Training for Sports* is based not only on a consensus of presently available scientific evidence, but also on many years of research, experience, coaching, and personal participation by the authors in amateur and professional sports. We hope that this book will increase your motivation and interest in cross-training and enable you to gain new insight into your overall training program for your primary sport.

part

I

CROSS-TRAINING PRINCIPLES

Cross-Training for Today's Athlete

The term *cross-training* means different things to different people. To some it may mean the effect that training on one side of the body has on the other. To other people it's an activity used to provide a break from a regular training program. We define cross-training as using another sport, activity, or training technique to help improve performance in the primary sport or activity. Downhill skiers often use bicycling during the summer months to maintain or improve the strength and endurance of their quadriceps (thighs) and improve their aerobic endurance. Golfers use abdominal and lower-back strength-training exercises to add power to their drives. Volleyball players use weight training to help them jump higher and put more power into their spike. Simply put, cross-training is a powerful training tool to help you gain the competitive edge in your primary sport and avoid two negative consequences of training we'll discuss later: overtraining and burnout.

BENEFITS OF CROSS-TRAINING

Cross-training offers tremendous improvements in your overall aerobic and anaerobic endurance, muscle strength and endurance, and flexibility and agility, all of which will improve the performance of your primary sport. These are some specific benefits of cross-training.

1. *Aerobic endurance.* Cross-training activities such as distance swimming, distance cycling, and aqua jogging (running or jogging in the water with a floatation vest) are very effective in increasing the ability of the cardiorespiratory system to supply oxygen to the working muscles. Nordic and Alpine skiers often use cycling and distance running during the off-season to maintain aerobic fitness.

2. *Anaerobic endurance.* For speed, sprinting, and power sports, where energy is needed to power short bursts of maximal performance, anaerobic endurance (endurance that relies on energy for stamina without requiring the presence of oxygen) is vital. Sports such as middle-distance swimming, middle-distance running, and wrestling are just a few examples of activities where the body depends on the energy stored in the muscles. Rowing machines, Versa Climber, and plyometrics are excellent cross-training activities for enhancing anaerobic endurance.

3. *Muscular strength.* Muscular strength and power provide the basis for the majority of sport activities, especially those that rely on quick, explosive movements. A number of cross-training activities that can overload the muscles by subjecting them to a greater-than-normal level of stress—such as stair climbing, weight training, and plyometrics—provide strength gains that athletes may not receive through training only in their primary sport.

4. *Muscular endurance.* Muscular endurance requires repetitive muscle contraction against a resistance for extended periods of time. This kind of repetitive movement is common in such sports as rowing, gymnastics, long sprints, wrestling, and swimming. As strength increases, there tends to be a corresponding increase in endurance. Increased strength will also result in the ability to increase the number of skilled repetitions. For example, in rowing, the ability to increase the number of strokes per unit of time is integral to success.

5. *Flexibility.* Almost all sports require good flexibility. Cross-training activities, such as yoga, ballet, or gymnastics, that require a wide range of joint movement or a specific stretching program can enhance flexibility. Flexibility exercises reduce the possibility of aches, pains, and inflammation associated with joints stressed through rigorous activity.

6. *Warm-up and cool-down exercises.* Warm-up and cool-down exercises help maximize the potential of each training period by preparing your body for vigorous activity. They also enhance your ability to recover from a long, hard workout by slowing the heart rate gradually and helping to prevent muscle injury and soreness.

7. *Injury prevention.* Strength improvements yield greater protection against injuries, particularly overuse injuries. Cross-training works muscle groups other than those needed in the primary sport or uses the primary sport's muscle groups in different patterns, allowing more areas to share the training stress and reducing stresses on muscles, tendons, ligaments, and bones.

8. *Injury rehabilitation.* Cross-training activities allow you to continue to train and prevent detraining when you cannot participate in your main sport due to an injury. Cross-training can even help to rehabilitate an injury. When specific limbs or joints have to be immobilized, strength and flexibility cross-training exercises can focus on other body parts—especially contralateral limbs—to help maintain muscle strength and range of motion. For example, exercise bicycle and deep- or shallow-water running are excellent activities for athletes who have injured their upper body, and arm ergometry, weight-resistance exercises that utilize only the arm and shoulder muscles, can be useful for those who have injured their lower body. For a body structure to heal properly it must not remain completely stationary. Movement (using flexibility and strength-training exercises) early after an injury is vital. Strength training through a full range of movement is required because improved levels of strength must be reached for each stage of rehabilitation and the eventual return to activity.

9. *Mental breaks.* Cross-training with other sports or activities provides a mental vacation without detraining or a loss of the fitness level. This can be very effective for breaking through the doldrums or plateaus in training. Variety can add spice to your fitness program and increase your motivation!

10. *Training extension.* Cross-training allows you to perform additional work within your primary sport with less risk of overtraining or injury. Suppose, for example, you are a distance runner who usually runs 35 to 40 miles a week effectively without injury. When you attempt to increase your mileage to 45 miles a week, however, you repeatedly become susceptible to overuse injury. In this situation, a cross-training program can help in several ways:

- Strength training can strengthen the problem, injury-prone areas, allowing them to better withstand additional training stress.
- Activities such as cycling or swimming can provide an additional endurance training stimulus with minimal or no additional stress to these problem areas.
- Warming up and cooling down with an activity such as bicycling can be a non-stressful way to improve training preparation and recovery.

POPULARITY OF CROSS-TRAINING

Cross-training has been used in one form or another throughout the history of sport. In ancient Greece, strength training was used to enhance athletic performance in the predominant sports of the day: discus, javelin, sprinting, and wrestling—all sports requiring speed, strength, and power.

Low-impact activities such as cycling are a great way to supplement your primary-sport training while decreasing your risk of overtraining or injury.

Over the years, a number of Olympic, professional, and amateur athletes have used cross-training to improve their performances. Along with swimmers and Alpine and Nordic skiers, baseball players have used cross-training to increase hitting power and speed. Because of the high physical demands encountered by triathletes training in three different sports, cross-training is an intregal part of their training regimens.

Today, athletes in a number of sports, from volleyball to wrestling, condition themselves with activities such as running and rope jumping. Athletes in almost all sports use weight or resistance training to improve their performance. Off-season cross-training programs help athletes maintain aerobic endurance and strength.

As the popularity of multisport events such as triathlon, duathlon, and biathlon has taken off, cross-training has evolved into a sophisticated method of training, with impressive results that enable athletes to compete in grueling events. Research in cross-training shows that humans can do much more exercise with greater workloads than ever imagined. Who would have thought 50 years ago that humans could swim 2.4 miles, bike 112 miles, and then run 26.2 miles in succession (Ironman Triathlon distance) and not only live through the experience, but do so with smiles on their faces? Many triathletes gain significant improvements in their major sport through cross-training with other sports, even when they have decreased their training in their primary sport.

Another development that has spurred cross-training's popularity is the coming-of-age of the Masters athlete. While there have always been a few hearty individuals who have continued to train and compete beyond their 30s (some even competing into their 80s and 90s), the ranks of older athletes are now burgeoning.

Lori Corbelli

A highly successful head volleyball coach for over 10 years, Lori Corbelli has been the recipient of both the West Coast Conference and Southwest Conference Coach of the Year awards and presently is head volleyball coach at Texas A&M University. Lori played for the United States Women's National Volleyball team from 1978 to 1984 and was a two time member of the U.S. Olympic Team. Lori lead the U.S. team in 1984 to a silver medal in the Los Angeles Olympics.

In 1987 she played Major League Volleyball for the San Jose Goldiggers. She was named the Most Valuable Player in the league's inaugural season. Laurie was also named MVP of the MLV's all-star game in 1989.

Lori believes cross-training to be a key ingredient in volleyball training. "Because we had such great success developing speed and strength in athletes with the National Team's cross-training program, I have used a significant number of cross-training techniques at Texas A&M. We are always in a strength building mode in our program and use supplemental activities such as sprints, agility, speed ladders, and shuttle runs to develop athletes' speed and explosiveness. Off-season, players spend an hour playing full-court basketball to work on their coordination, stamina, and aggressiveness. We also make sure that stretching is done daily to ensure increased flexibility and to help prevent injury. Athletes also use the StairMaster and bike for low-impact aerobic improvement. We utilize gymnastic, endurance jumping circuits, and agility circuits. The circuits are both aerobic- or anaerobic-oriented. We also incorporate plyometrics using jump boxes, resistance bands, and bounding.

Cross-training has been extremely important in my own personal development as an Olympic volleyball player. I certainly see great benefits in my own program at Texas A&M University and will continue to use cross-training to develop athletes I coach in the future."

Although older athletes can often handle a large volume of training, they need a longer period of time to recover from hard workouts or races. Therefore, many of the world's best Masters runners have turned to cross-training as a way to continue to train while recovering from tough competitions. Many of these athletes, who previously had run seven days a week for years, now run only four days each week and supplement this training with three days of cycling, swimming, or aqua jogging. This allows the leg muscles to be exercised while reducing the debilitating impact forces associated with running on an everyday basis. Many of these runners improve their performance while running less and cross-training more.

A third major impetus for the increasing popularity of cross-training has been the growing numbers of casual athletes. While the overall number of runners has decreased from the high-water mark of the late 1970s, the number of adults participating in fitness pursuits has increased. The area of greatest increase is in aerobic exercise, such as aerobic dance and step aerobics. Many previously sedentary individuals are going to athletic clubs and enjoying the benefits of being physically fit.

Cross-training can help you on your way toward mastering performance by giving you the competitive edge.

CROSS-TRAINING AND YOU

Every athlete enjoys achievement and the satisfaction of bettering his or her performance: swimming or rowing just a little faster, hitting the ball just a little bit farther. The sense of mastery, the accomplishment of a task or goal that once seemed difficult, can boost self-confidence and general well-being. The desire to be witness to and to control your environment—to enjoy it, to react to it, and to master it—is the most significant factor in providing satisfaction. Cross-training can help you on your way toward becoming a stronger, more powerful athlete.

If you are a casual athlete not interested in competitive sports, your goals will vary from those of the competitor. Cross-training will introduce you to a number of challenging activities that you probably have not explored. Even though the volume and intensity of your training may be less than those involved in competitive sports, you will still receive many of the same physical and psychological benefits cross-training has to offer.

Cross-training is the training trend of the present and future. Our goal with this book is to provide you with the information and understanding necessary to set up a cross-training program that allows you to maximize your potential. Part I covers the essentials of cross-training, from training principles, activities, and equipment to information on how to integrate cross-training into your overall training program. Part II presents sport-specific cross-training recommendations and exercises geared toward optimizing your conditioning and level of performance in your primary sport. Enjoy!

chapter 2

Cross-Training for Aerobic and Anaerobic Endurance

Sports and activities vary widely in the amounts of energy they require and how fast that energy is needed. Activities such as long-distance running and swimming require lesser amounts of immediate energy, but this energy must be delivered over a long period of time. These sports are considered aerobic because they rely heavily upon the body's aerobic energy system. Activities such as sprinting and weight lifting, on the other hand, require large amounts of energy in a very short period of time. These are fueled by the body's anaerobic energy system. Some activities such as soccer, racquet sports, and basketball draw upon both energy systems.

If you're looking to improve your aerobic and anaerobic endurance, there's plenty out there to help you do it. A runner might use aqua jogging or an exercise bike to help increase aerobic endurance without subjecting herself to the constant impact shock inherent in running on the roads. A tennis player might use the cross-country ski machine or the StairMaster for his warm-up or cool-down to enhance the quality and intensity of his tennis training. Before taking a look at which conditioning exercises or equipment may be best for your program, let's go over some basics regarding aerobic and anaerobic exercise and energy.

AEROBIC EXERCISE

Aerobic (or cardiorespiratory) endurance is the ability of the body to supply oxygen and energy to the cells and remove waste products in order to sustain prolonged rhythmical exercise. This is accomplished by the heart pumping oxygenated blood through the arteries to the cells. At the cellular level, oxygen is absorbed by the cells, and waste products are removed and carried away by the blood. An adequate supply of oxygen prevents the buildup of lactic acid, which produces fatigue in the muscle, and also allows for the production of adenosine triphosphate (ATP)—the basic energy source in the muscle. The heart then pumps this blood to the lungs to be re-oxygenated and returned to the heart via the pulmonary veins to begin the systemic circulation cycle once again.

Typical aerobic exercises that use large-muscle groups are distance running, bicycling, cross-country skiing, and swimming. These activities, although strenuous, are rhythmical and are performed at less than all-out intensity. During aerobic exercise, there is a brief rest period for the main working muscle group (during which another muscle group does the work) while the bloodstream brings nutrients to the resting muscle cells and removes metabolic wastes. This allows the movement to continue for a long period of time.

The most accurate way to evaluate your aerobic endurance is to determine your body's capacity to consume oxygen at a maximum rate (maximum oxygen uptake) from the total amount taken in. Maximum oxygen uptake (VO_2max) is a measure of the amount of oxygen used by the cells during strenuous exercise per unit of time and indicates how efficiently your heart, lungs, and cell metabolism are functioning. Aerobic sports require much higher levels of VO_2 because of the need to supply oxygen to the muscles. Along with direct measurements in a laboratory, there are a number of field tests, such as the 1.5-mile run presented next, which can measure VO_2max indirectly.

Testing Your Aerobic Fitness

The 1.5-mile run should be attempted only if you are in good enough condition to run this distance. If not, you should consult a physician or other fitness specialist.

1.5-Mile Run.   The 1.5-mile run is an easy test that can be done on an oval track or a straightaway. If you become overtired while running this distance, shift down to a slow jog or walk. Do not unduly stress yourself. Keep track of the amount of time it takes you to run the 1.5 miles, then find your fitness level in table 2.1.

Table 2.1   Aerobic Fitness Guidelines for the 1.5-Mile Test

Fitness Category		Age (years)		
		13-19	20-29	30-39
I. Very poor	(men)	>15:31*	>16:01	>16:31
	(women)	>18:31	>19:01	>19:31
II. Poor	(men)	12:11-15:30	14:01-16:00	14:44-16:30
	(women)	16:55-18:30	18:31-19:00	19:01-19:30
III. Average	(men)	10:49-12:10	12:01-14:00	12:31-14:45
	(women)	14:31-16:54	15:55-18:30	16:31-19:00
IV. Good	(men)	9:41-10:48	10:46-12:00	11:01-12:30
	(women)	12:30-14:30	13:31-15:54	14:31-16:30
V. Excellent	(men)	8:37- 9:40	9:45-10:45	10:00-11:00
	(women)	11:50-12:29	12:30-13:30	13:00-14:30
VI. Superior	(men)	<8:37	<9:45	<10:00
	(women)	<11:50	<12:30	<13:00
Fitness Category		**Age (years)**		
		40-49	50-59	60+
I. Very poor	(men)	>17:31	>19:01	>20:01
	(women)	>20:01	>20:31	>21:01
II. Poor	(men)	15:36-17:30	17:01-19:00	19:01-20:00
	(women)	19:31-20:00	20:01-20:30	21:00-21:31
III. Average	(men)	13:01-15:35	14:31-17:00	16:16-19:00
	(women)	17:31-19:30	19:01-20:00	19:31-20:30
IV. Good	(men)	11:31-13:00	12:31-14:30	14:00-16:15
	(women)	15:56-17:30	16:31-19:00	17:31-19:30
V. Excellent	(men)	10:30-11:30	11:30-12:30	11:15-13:59
	(women)	13:45-15:55	14:30-16:30	16:30-17:30
VI. Superior	(men)	<10:30	<11:00	<11:15
	(women)	<13:45	<14:30	<16:30

*< Means "less than"; > means "more than."
Reprinted from Cooper 1982.

Increasing Your Aerobic Endurance

To increase your aerobic endurance, it is necessary to exercise at a level of intensity that is high enough to cause physical adaptation, an increase in the ability of the heart and lungs to deliver oxygen to the working muscles, to occur. An effective way of determining exercise intensity is to monitor your heart rate. This approach is referred to as a *threshold effect* or *training heart rate effect*. Research has shown that a training level of 70 percent of your maximum heart rate, or approximately 60 percent of your $\dot{V}O_2$max level, is considered to be a minimal level of intensity necessary to increase aerobic endurance. Although intensity may vary from athlete to athlete, it has been found that intensities between 80 to 90 percent of maximum oxygen uptake are optimal for increasing aerobic endurance (figure 2.1). For more on intensity and increasing your aerobic endurance, see page 13.

Determining your training target heart rate (the rate at which your heart should be beating for aerobic training benefit) is relatively simple. First you estimate your maximum heart rate (the maximum rate at which your heart can beat according to your age) by subtracting your age from 220. While this method is valid, it is not an exact measure because the formula *predicts* rather than *assesses*. As a result, there is a possibility of about a 10 beats-per-minute (bpm) error. Next subtract your resting pulse rate (heart rate taken at rest) from your predicted maximum heart rate. Your resting pulse rate can be determined by taking your pulse in the morning before you get out of bed, averaged over three to five days. Now, multiply the difference by 70 percent. This is your minimal threshold for training. Add this product to your resting heart rate and the result will give you your target heart rate. See Table 2.2 for a sample worksheet to help you calculate your target heart rate.

When measuring your heart rate, take your pulse either by placing a hand directly over your heart, touching the radial artery at the base of your thumb, or on the temple artery in front of your ear. Take your pulse for 15 seconds and multiply by four to determine the one-minute rate.

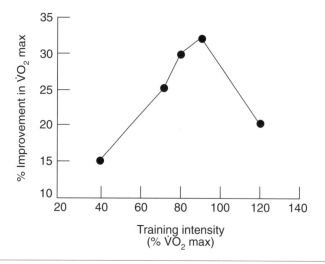

Figure 2.1   Relationship between training intensity and percent improvement in $\dot{V}O_2$max.

The following is an example of determining the target heart rate level for a 20-year-old individual with a resting heart rate of 65 bpm:

220 - 20 = 200 bpm (est. maximum heart rate)
200 - 65 = 135 (again, 65 is the resting heart rate in this example)
135 x .70 = 94.5 (.70 [70 percent] is the desired intensity)
94.5 + 65 = 159.5 (approx. 160) bpm (target heart rate)

Table 2.2   Calculating Your Training Target Heart Rate (TTHR)

1. Maximum Heart Rate = 220 beats/min – _____ = beats/min.
   age in years

2. TTHR = _____ – _____ × .7 + _____ = _____
   your maximum   your resting   your resting   beats/min.
   heart rate   heart rate   heart rate

ANAEROBIC EXERCISE

Anaerobic activities are those where the oxygen demands of the muscles are so high that the circulatory system cannot supply adequate amounts of oxygen quickly enough. The muscles can continue to function (for a short time) by using chemical processes that bypass the aerobic energy system.

Briefly, here's how it works: With the stimulation of exercise, energy-rich compounds stored in the muscles—adenosine triphosphate (ATP) and phospho-creatine (PC)—are broken down to release the immediate energy necessary for muscle contraction. Because only small amounts of these compounds are stored in the muscles, energy from ATP and PC is only available for a brief period of time. Another source of energy—sugar—is stored in the muscles as well in the form of glycogen. When glycogen is broken down, the released energy produces more ATP for the muscles to use. When glycogen is burned in the absence of oxygen, however, it produces a byproduct known as *lactic acid*, which helps to cause muscle fatigue. For this reason, the anaerobic energy system is limited to activities that last from one to two minutes. "All-out" sports like sprinting, arm wrestling, shot putting, and weight lifting that require large bursts of energy make use of the anaerobic energy system.

Testing for anaerobic endurance is more difficult than testing for aerobic endurance due to the unique demands each sport places on the body and the need for special equipment and testing protocols. The Wingate anaerobic test, a bicycle ergometer test that measures anaerobic power and capacity, is often used to determine anaerobic endurance levels.

Increasing Your Anaerobic Endurance

To increase anaerobic endurance, it's important to train using all-out explosive activities (such as sprint running, swimming, or cycling) for 10 seconds to 2 minutes in duration at 85 to 100 percent of maximum effort. These can either be done as *speed work*, where you do an activity of short duration (e.g., running 100-400 meters) at a very high intensity, then rest, or by using *interval training*, where you alternate short periods of high-intensity training (30 seconds to 2 minutes) with short periods of slow, recovery pace training (2-15 minutes). The number of intervals you do and the number of sessions you spend a week on anaerobic training will depend on the energy requirements for your particular sport and your training schedule. To see how a sample long-distance runner might put interval training to work, see page 76.

COMBINING AEROBIC AND ANAEROBIC ENERGY SYSTEMS

When performing most activities, both energy systems, aerobic and anaerobic, are called upon in varying degrees; however, the oxygen needs of anaerobic athletes are much different than athletes participating in aerobic sports.

Consider the case of a 100-meter sprinter who depends on the energy-rich compounds (ATP and PC) stored in the muscles and released to provide energy to explode down the track. Only after the race, when the sprinter gasps for air, does she rely heavily on the aerobic system to help her return from the anaerobic state to reach homeostasis (equilibrium). The long-distance cyclist, on the other hand, relies heavily on the aerobic energy system to supply energy during a long, grueling road race but also must draw upon anaerobic energy when riding up steep hills or sprinting with the pack to the finish line.

Each sport or activity places demands on the body's energy systems to different degrees, and it is important that your overall training reflect this mix. Figure 2.2 shows the approximate aerobic and anaerobic energy requirements of different sports. For more on the aerobic and anaerobic emphasis of training, see page 26.

The sprint element found in many long-distance sports requires you to develop both aerobic and anaerobic endurance.

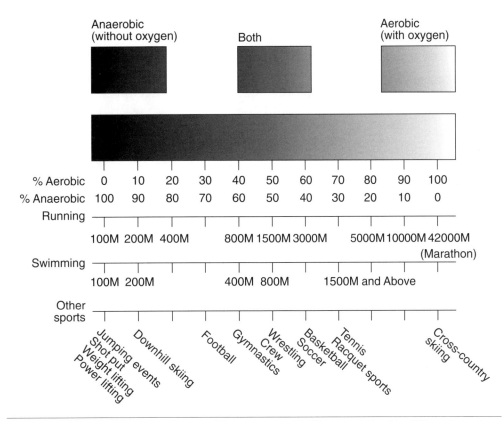

Figure 2.2   Relative amounts of anaerobic versus aerobic fitness required in different sports. Reprinted from Hatfield 1985.

EXERCISE PRESCRIPTION

Before embarking on an aerobic or anaerobic exercise program, you must be aware of three important principles: *intensity, time* (duration), and *frequency*. Intensity refers to the workload, or level of the exercise; duration is the amount of time utilized for each exercise session; and frequency is the number of exercise sessions per week. Generally, and within limits, the more intensive, the longer, and the more frequent the training program, the greater the aerobic and anaerobic benefits.

Intensity

As previously mentioned, for a training effect to occur within the cardiorespiratory and muscle systems, the exercise program must consist of activities that produce an overload on these systems. For aerobic training, the intensity level should be between 70 to 90 percent of the maximum heart rate reserve and be maintained throughout the exercise period. Most competitive endurance athletes work close to the 85- and 90-percent level. If you have been sedentary for some time you should start at the 60-percent level. Your desired exercise intensity should be gauged by your age and relative fitness. An exercise pulse rate of 110 to 120 bpm for middle-age individuals may be an effective training stimulus, whereas younger people may have to work at a steady pulse rate of 140 to 160 bpm. Be aware that high-intensity levels of exercise may lead to overtraining problems. See chapter 5 for special recommendations on the prevention of overtraining.

6	No exertion at all
7	Extremely light
8	
9	Very light
10	
11	Light
12	
13	Somewhat hard
14	
15	Hard
16	
17	Very hard
18	
19	Extremely hard
20	Maximal exertion

Figure 2.3 Borg's Rating of Perceived Exertion (RPE) scale.
Reprinted from Borg, 1985.

Another way of measuring intensity is to monitor various body sensations, such as body temperature, breathing intensity, and muscle and joint sensations in order to arrive at a subjective (or perceived) level of intensity. Researcher Gunnar Borg developed a model that correlates heart rate with this approach to perceiving exertion. His Rating of Perceived Exertion (RPE) model (see figure 2.3) rates perceived exertion on a graded scale of 6 to 20, 6 being a resting level (no exertion at all); and 20, maximal exertion. Multiplying your perceived exertion number by a factor of 10 corresponds to your actual heart rate at that level of perceived intensity. For example, if during exercise you perceive your level of intensity as 15 (hard), then your heart rate should be at 150 bpm.

Time (Duration)

How long you exercise depends primarily on the intensity of the exercise and your long-range goals. Beginners should exercise for a minimum of 15 to 20 minutes for each exercise session. As fitness level improves, the exercise session can be increased to 30 minutes or more. Maintaining your target training level during the 30 minutes of exercise will improve your cardiorespiratory endurance; for anaerobic exercise, concentrate on short intervals of higher-intensity training.

Frequency

You do not have to train seven days a week to achieve aerobic and anaerobic benefit. Working out three to five days a week is very productive for increasing fitness. It is true that many competitive endurance athletes train five to seven days a week. One of the dangers of such a high frequency of training, however, is overtraining, which can result in fatigue, decreased performance, and/or injury. Cross-training can prevent the overtraining of one particular muscle group by spreading the workload to other muscle groups. By using cross-training methods, one can substitute running, cycling, StairMaster, ski machines, and other activities to help prevent overtraining.

There is substantial variability in determining the intensity and volume of exercise for athletes. The most talented performers may not necessarily be the ones with the greatest capacity to endure periods of overtraining. Also, athletes of similar capacities may respond differently to a standard training regimen. For example, Mark Spitz, who won seven Olympic gold medals, never swam more than 10,000 yards a day. On the other hand, Vladimir Salnikov, another accomplished, world-class swimmer, regularly swam close to 22,000 yards a day while in training. Some athletes benefit from intensive training where others are vulnerable. Thus, a particular training schedule may improve the performance of one athlete, be insufficient for another, and prove detrimental to yet a third.

Many sports now require year-round workouts; consequently, off-seasons become even shorter. Sports such as tennis, gymnastics, and swimming continue

Knowing your training limits helps you avoid complications caused by overtraining: poor performance, fatigue, and burnout.

throughout the year with little off-season time. In addition, the increased intensity of the training loads carried by some athletes is so demanding that it often limits rather than enhances performance. Basketball, football, baseball, and soccer seasons are now so long that there is little break between the end of one season and the start of training for the next.

Increasing Intensity, Duration, and Frequency

There are two ways that you can determine the appropriate times to increase intensity (load), duration, and frequency. One method is to rely on your own past experience or listen to the expertise of your coaches. A second, more reliable method is to base your training on the monitoring of your heart rate. The underlying principle is, as the body adapts to training, resting heart rate and exercise heart rates for a given load will be reduced. Eventually a plateau will be reached where there is no longer a reduction in heart rate for a given load no matter how long one trains (a hereditary limit has probably been reached). Even if you reach a limit of maximum oxygen uptake, you can still enhance the ability to work longer at a greater percentage of your maximum oxygen uptake. In order to do this, you must work at high levels of intensity and elicit higher heart rates if you want to continue improving the capacity to persist in exercise at a higher percentage of your maximum oxygen uptake.

After a few weeks of training at a given intensity, you may find that you don't need to exercise at a faster rate, or with a heavier load, to attain the same exercise heart rate. At this time you can be fairly certain you've reached a heart rate plateau.

ANATOMY OF A WORKOUT

It is important that every workout contain a warm-up and cool-down in addition to the main exercise. A good warm-up prepares the muscles, tendons, and ligaments for action. It gets the blood circulating, raises the core body temperature, and enhances flexibility. The more intense the exercise activity, the greater the need for a proper warm-up. Many types and combinations of aerobic activities can be used in a warm-up: running, cycling, stair climbing, and so on. Choose one or more that you enjoy. A good warm-up should last about 10 to 15 minutes and include slowing down to stretch after you begin to break a sweat.

Following a rigorous workout—aerobic or anaerobic—you should continue to exercise at a low intensity (stretching and walking 10 to 15 minutes). This step will allow your body to adjust to a resting state. Cooling down prevents the blood from pooling in the lower extremities, which could reduce the amount of blood returning to the heart and disrupt the cardiac cycle. Cooling down also helps reduce muscle soreness, dizziness, and the amount of biochemical fatigue products, such as lactic acid, that build up in the blood.

Exercise Guidelines

The American College of Sports Medicine makes the following recommendations for the quality and quantity of training for developing and maintaining cardiorespiratory fitness and body composition in the healthy adult:

1. Frequency of training—three to five days per week.

2. Intensity of training—60 to 90 percent of maximum heart rate.

3. Duration of training—15 to 60 minutes of continuous aerobic activity. Duration depends on the intensity of the activity; thus, lower-intensity activity should be conducted over a longer period of time. Because of the importance of the total fitness effect and the fact that it is more readily attained in programs of longer duration, and because of the potential hazards and compliance problems associated with high-intensity activity, lower- to moderate-intensity activity of longer duration is recommended for the nonathletic adult.

4. Mode of activity—Any activity that uses large-muscle groups that can be maintained continuously and is rhythmical and aerobic in nature (e.g., running, jogging, walking, hiking, swimming, skating, bicycling, rowing, cross-country skiing, rope skipping, and various endurance game activities).

EXERCISE PRECAUTIONS

The American College of Sports Medicine's and the American Medical Association's pre-exercise guidelines recommend that healthy individuals under 30 years of age do not need a pre-exercise medical clearance. They do recommend medical clearance, however, before embarking on an exercise program. Individuals over 30 years of age do not need medical clearance if they feel they are in good shape. However, regardless of age, those who have any cardiovascular disorders, diabetes, bone and joint disease, or other chronic diseases, or exhibit risk factors related to these medical problems should seek medical approval prior to participating in an exercise program. In addition, if a pregnant woman has medical problems, any sort of disease, or other complications, she should seek advice from her obstetrician before undertaking or continuing an exercise program.

It's important to be familiar with the following exercise precautions before beginning your cross-training exercise program:

1. Have a thorough physical examination done before you begin.

2. If fatigue lasts two hours or more following an exercise session, the program is too rigorous. Reduce your level of exercise. Be careful not to confuse fatigue with muscle soreness, which generally appears 24 to 48 hours after exercise and lasts for a few days.

3. Alcohol and exercise do not mix. Alcohol can result in dehydration and can inhibit cardiac output.

4. Cigarette smoking limits oxygen exchange in the lungs, causing shortness of breath and limiting your level of fitness attainment.

5. Use your heart rate as a guide to the intensity of the exercise.

6. Sporadic exercise may actually be detrimental to your health if done at too high an intensity. Three to five exercise sessions a week are minimal for optimum benefit. One or two low-intensity exercise sessions a week may be beneficial in burning extra calories, but will have little effect on fitness levels except for the elderly, or individuals who are sedentary or unfit.

ENDURANCE EXERCISES AND EQUIPMENT

There are many new exercise machines available, and with them, a greater number of activities to choose from to help build your aerobic and anaerobic endurance. The following sections describe different exercises and exercise equipment and some advantages and disadvantages of each.

Aerobics

Aerobics, or aerobic dance, started originally as a method of performing calisthenics exercises to music. Later, aerobics incorporated other exercises and dance movements to music and is continuing to evolve. Classes are now offered that focus on step aerobics, low- and nonimpact aerobics, interval aerobics, aerobics

Exercise During Pregnancy

No scientific evidence supports the old theory that pregnant women who exercise rigorously develop tense abdominal muscles, which result in problems during delivery. On the contrary, some evidence indicates that women who are athletic have easier labor and fewer undesirable side effects during delivery. If a pregnant woman has medical problems, disease, or other complications, she should seek advice from her obstetrician before undertaking or continuing an exercise program. Extremely rigorous activities that require prolonged endurance or produce a large oxygen debt are discouraged since they could result in reduced oxygen in the circulatory system and an increase in the internal body temperature of the mother and the fetus. Rhythmic, moderate activity, however, is well advised and safe for both mother and fetus. A program of 30 minutes of exercise three times a week is recommended. The following are exercise guidelines during pregnancy:

1. Exercise intensity should not go beyond the 70 percent threshold level. The American College of Obstetricians and Gynecologists cautions against heart rates exceeding 140 beats per minute. However, prepregnancy fitness level is probably a better predictor of maximum allowable heart rate than 140 beats per minute.

2. Exercise should be stopped if there is any pain or bleeding.
3. Adequate intakes of iron, calcium, and vitamins should be maintained before and during pregnancy.
4. Avoid rigorous exercise at high altitudes.
5. Avoid bouncing, jarring, and twisting activities that put your abdomen in jeopardy.
6. If you feel very tired or experience discomfort or unusual symptoms, stop and rest.
7. You should not exercise so intensely that you are unable to talk.
8. Don't exercise while lying on your back after the fourth month; this can block blood supply to the uterus and depress fetal heart rate. If you need to rest, lie on your side.
9. Don't exercise rigorously in hot, humid weather. (Core body temperature should not go above 101 degrees Fahrenheit.) Avoid hot tubs and saunas.
10. Always drink plenty of water before, during, and after exercise.
11. Your exercise program should be started well in advance of pregnancy.
12. Research is not confirmed in the area of the detrimental effects of a pregnant mother being inverted as in such activities as gymnastics and yoga.

for pregnant women, stretching, and muscle strength and endurance. The greatest change in recent years has been the increasing number of men and athletes from other sports who are using aerobics for exercise and cross-training. The variability of intensity in these classes is quite large and tends to reflect the personality and goals of the instructor: high energy, relaxing, etc. Most health clubs have enough variety in instructors and types of classes that you should be able to find one that fits your fitness level, goals, interests, and personality.

Agility Exercises

Agility exercises, such as obstacle or zigzag running, or ball balancing, are discussed in chapter 4. What's important to note here is that these exercises can be used as part of an aerobic, anaerobic, or interval workout circuit.

Arm Ergometry

Arm ergometry is basically arm cycling or using a bicycle-type device for the upper extremity. The upper body ergometer (UBE) has been used quite successfully for some time by athletes with lower extremity disabilities or injuries. Because of the range of resistance settings, it can be used in a number of ways: aerobically, anaerobically, for interval training, and for muscular endurance and strength development. The UBE can be used in both a clockwise or counterclockwise direction and is a useful cross-training tool for athletes who rely heavily on their arms, such as kayakers, boxers, racquet sports athletes, cross-country skiers, swimmers, wrestlers, triathletes, and those in the martial arts.

Aqua Aerobics

Aqua aerobics is somewhat similar to dance aerobics in that flexibility and cardiorespiratory endurance are emphasized. There may be some gains in muscular endurance and strength if some hydroresistant devices such as gloves or paddles are used during the class.

Aqua Jogging

There are several ways to aqua jog. One is to simply run in the water with the water providing its own resistance. The water level can be manipulated in some pools to allow for varying resistance (simply move yourself into deeper water for more resistance). Another method is to move your legs through the water to mimic running or another lower or upper extremity action in a similar manner to aqua aerobics. An increasingly popular and very effective method is to use a flotation vest that allows you to float vertically in the water. With the vest you can simulate running quite effectively but without the impact shock. For this reason it has become a very popular rehabilitation method for injured runners and other athletes.

Bicycling: Stationary, Road, and Mountain

The stationary bicycle is the most versatile of cross-training equipment as it allows for great variations of intensity levels by adjusting the tension or resistance. The exercise bike can be used for aerobic work (low resistance), anaerobic work (mid to high resistance), interval training (alternating low and high settings), as well as muscular endurance work using very high resistance. It is also an excellent device for warm-up and cool-down exercises (low settings) and for rehabilitation, particularly for lower extremity overtraining injuries associated with impact shock. The disadvantage of cycling is that it places stress on the knees in susceptible individuals. This stress can be reduced if the rider uses a high-seat setting, with knees near full extension when the foot is at the bottom of the stroke. A second knee-stress reducer is to use light resistance and a faster cycling pace as opposed to heavy resistance with fewer cycles per minute (cpm). We recommend at least 50 cpm or higher for aerobic fitness training. Most triathletes train at 75 to 90 cpm and some cycling track racers are able to cycle at 120 cpm and higher and still maintain good cycling mechanics. If you have a road or mountain bike, you can adapt these as exercise bikes for indoor use by using a bike stand such as a turbo trainer or magnetic trainer. This precludes having to buy an exercise bike for foul weather. In fair weather, you can choose from either indoor or outdoor road or trail training.

Cross-Country Ski Machine

The cross-country ski machine involves both upper and lower extremities and aerobic endurance. Another advantage is that it can be used indoors and at home. One slight disadvantage is that some people find the machine takes a little while to get used to; the movements can initially feel awkward.

Flexibility Exercises

Flexibility exercises are presented in chapter 4. They are mentioned here to remind you that lack of flexibility (the ability to move smoothly through the range of motion needed for your sport) can result in a decrease in performance. In running, for example, chronically tight hamstrings can cause the hip flexors to work disproportionately harder, particularly at fast or racing speeds, thus reducing performance. Good flexibility can also be beneficial for boxers and weight lifters by increasing their range of joint movement, thus preventing injuries to muscles and tendons, which may be stressed by awkward and unexpected movements. Flexibility aids the tennis player in efficient trunk rotation and is equally essential for the baseball player to protect against shoulder and elbow injury in the throwing arm.

Lateral Movement Sports

Lateral movement sports, such as racquetball, basketball, and tennis, involve lateral movement as well as forward and backward movement. This is in comparison with running, swimming, or cycling, which are primarily single-plane, forward movements. Performing lateral sports keeps the muscles that produce side and backward motion fit and strong. This helps maintain overall body strength and endurance and helps prevent injury. It can also help increase performance in other single-plane sports because some large-muscle groups used in lateral sports are used heavily in single-plane sports (such as the thigh adductor muscles [groin muscles] in running). Participating occasionally in lateral sports has the added benefit of being an enjoyable alternative to boredom or overtraining.

Plyometrics

This form of exercise is covered in chapter 3 as these anaerobic exercises requiring explosive movements are primarily used for strength and power development.

Roller Blading

While roller blading has become increasingly popular in recent years in the United States, it has been used for more than 20 years as a dryland cross-training method for speed skaters in Russia. Most enthusiasts roller blade for fun and cardiorespiratory training, but this activity may also be used by the cross-trainer for anaerobic and interval training. Its main advantage is the absence of impact shock. Of course, this is only true if you do not fall and impact the pavement! For this reason, we highly recommend protective equipment and developing your skating and stopping skills before approaching Warp 1 (high) speeds. This is an excellent cross-training method for runners, cross-country skiers (especially skate-style skiers), ice hockey players, and speed skaters.

Rope Jumping

Rope jumping is one of the oldest cross-training activities in sports and has been used by boxers and other athletes since the later 19th century. It can, with variations in speed, technique, and rope weight, be used as an aerobic, anaerobic, or interval exercise. It may also be used as a warm-up activity or to enhance balance. Using the newer type of heavy ropes can increase the upper body workout if so desired.

Rowing Machine

The rowing machine allows for a near full-body workout. Most rowing machines take up little space and are easily moveable, which enhances home use. Some of the home machines can be used for additional exercises by reversing your position on the seat and performing pushing movements for the pectoral muscles.

Running

Running is the most common activity found across the sport spectrum. If you enjoy running, it makes an excellent cross-training exercise. Remember, running can be done in varied directions: forward, backward, sideways, and shuffling (as is done in basketball, tennis, and football). If your sport includes these variations of running, you might want to consider using some of these movements in your cross-training in either an aerobic, anaerobic, or interval capacity.

Stair-Stepping Machine (StairMaster)

The success and popularity of the StairMaster machine has surprised many people in the fitness business because the anticipated high level of boredom expected with its use has not been vocalized. It is a very popular—often the most popular—machine at many health clubs. Although some exercise scientists expected a large dropout rate among users due to knee pain, this has not been the case to any large extent. So, why not give this equipment a try? If you use longer steps rather than short, quick steps, you will work your gluteal (butt) muscles harder during the exercise. Another tip is to remain upright during the activity, rather than leaning over or resting your forearms on the support bars. This will give you a better, more biomechanically sound workout.

Swimming

Swimming is an excellent full-body exercise that has certain cross-training advantages: there is no impact shock as in running, and it can be used to lengthen or increase flexibility of muscles (such as the hamstrings, which are shortened in running and cycling). Plus, it is a perfect hot weather exercise that eliminates heat stress and hyperthermia. In cold water, a wet suit can be used to prevent hypothermia. The one disadvantage of swimming is that proper technique is essential. If you are not a good swimmer, try taking lessons or joining a swim club to improve your stroke technique. It's important to note that individuals will have a lower heart rate when swimming at the same intensity as running because the horizontal position distributes the blood more uniformly; and the water helps to dissipate heat more rapidly, thus reducing the workload on the heart. The difference between running and swimming is approximately 13 bpm. This difference must be subtracted from the age-related maximum heart rate if swimming is your main means of training. Thus, a 40-year-old swimmer would subtract 40 plus 13 from 220 to get a maximum heart rate of 167 when computing the training effect. For running, the maximum heart rate would be 180.

Treadmill

The treadmill is found in almost all of the larger health clubs or can be purchased for a reasonable price for home use. The advantage of a treadmill is its convenience: You can easily avoid stormy, inclement weather or hot, humid conditions by using the treadmill indoors. In many areas and especially for women, running at night can be risky, thus the treadmill also has a safety component. Most treadmills have a height elevation feature that can be helpful if you are training for races on hilly terrain (e.g., the Boston Marathon and its infamous Heartbreak Hill) but live in the flatlands and have no hill training sites available.

Some people have little or no access to a track and have difficulty doing interval training. Many of the better treadmills can be programmed to mimic interval training by programming, for example, a 75-second quarter mile followed by a 2-minute quarter mile pace. Many of these treadmills can be set up to provide a fully programmed workout with a warm-up, gradual increased pace, training pace, and cool-down. You can also program hills and a short, high-tempo pace at regular or irregular intervals to mimic trail running.

The major disadvantage of the treadmill is that the scenery remains constant. In a club, they are often placed so as to provide as much viewing interest as possible or sometimes come equipped with magazines in easy reach and/or earphones for stereo or television. At home, placing the treadmill near a window or in front of a television can alleviate boredom. For some people, the treadmill requires a brief adjustment period before they become comfortable.

Some control features found in treadmills include the following:

- Speed: The treadmill should allow you to run up to 10 to 15 miles per hour (mph). Fifteen mph is a 4-minute per mile pace (60-second quarter mile pace) and is not necessary for most athletes; however, it will allow the

Stephen Negoesco

Steve Negoesco is the first NCAA soccer coach to post his 500th collegiate career victory, including four NCAA championship victories and two runners-up. To date, he's had 525 victories, 63 ties and only one losing season.

Negoesco has taught soccer to thousands of young athletes in California. In 1953 he established the San Francisco Youth Soccer Program. In 1961 he coached a junior team to a national championship. His San Francisco Athletic Club team won the National Open Cup in 1975. This year he conducted the Third Annual Steve Negoesco Soccer Academy exclusively for coaches of the sport.

An escapee from a German concentration camp in his youth, Negoesco was a member of the Romanian National team and an All-American soccer player at the University of San Francisco.

"Because high-level competitive soccer now requires a year-round training regimen, it is vital for the athlete to use cross-training exercises, not only during the competitive season, but during the off-season. Cross-training in the off-season can be used to develop and maintain cardiorespiratory endurance and muscle strength. Cross-training is also a valuable aid in rehabilitation and maintaining fitness in injured players. We use weight training for rehabilitation and muscle strength and endurance. We also use a variety of cross-training methods such as the StairMaster, agility drills, plyometrics, and sprint and distance running for aerobic conditioning. I have found that if athletes are offered a variety of cross-training options for maintaining fitness, it increases their motivation, reduces boredom, and in some cases limits staleness in training."

accomplished runner to do interval training. A 10-mph treadmill (6-minute per mile pace or 75-second quarter mile pace) will be sufficient for almost everyone in a club setting. The 10-mph speed will likely be used by only a few members. A slow speed capability is also important for walkers and for cardiac and injury rehabilitation.

- Elevation: An elevation feature is desirable for walkers, hikers, and runners.
- Reverse: A reverse feature unique to treadmills allows for downhill training for walkers, hikers, and runners.

Versa Climber

A Versa Climber is a device that simulates a climbing action similar to climbing a telephone pole that has hand and foot pegs. This exercise works both the upper and lower extremities, although you can modify its use to emphasize one over the other.

The rate at which you can work the machine is somewhat variable; however, even at a slow rate it is a challenging exercise. At a fast rate with long steps and arm pulls it is an anaerobic exercise for even a very fit individual. Herein lies the uniqueness of the machine in that you can use the machine to get a full-body anaerobic or aerobic workout, or to provide a brisk full-body warm-up. This can be an especially effective exercise for rock climbers as well as a cross-training exercise for runners, swimmers, and rowers.

Weight Training/Resistance Training

Weight training is primarily used for developing strength and muscular endurance and is covered in chapter 3. You should be aware, however, that weight training can be used as a cardiorespiratory activity if very light weight and medium to high repetitions are used—especially if arranged as circuit training (where one goes from one station to another with little or no rest in between). Each individual repetition, or rep, should still be done in a slow, controlled fashion when working toward aerobic benefits.

TRAINING PROGRAMS FOR AEROBIC AND ANAEROBIC ENDURANCE

As previously mentioned, your aerobic program must include continuous, long duration, sustained activity between 70 to 90 percent of your maximum heart rate reserve, at least three times a week (and not more than six), and 20 to 60 minutes in duration per workout. The activity should be rhythmic, involving large-muscle group activity. It is vital to overload these specific muscle groups in order to facilitate oxygen transport to the muscles being trained. For example, aerobic arm exercises are extremely beneficial for swimmers, paddlers, and rowers.

As one would expect, resistance training is not very effective in increasing aerobic endurance. The only exception might be found in untrained individuals. Athletes involved in running activities can cross-train with other aerobic activities such as cycling, swimming, deep-water running, and the StairMaster. A cautionary note: Deep-water running may place a slightly greater load on the anaerobic system than does land running.

Activities such as football, baseball, basketball, volleyball, and sprint sports require strength and power. Athletes in these sports should therefore focus less on aerobic training and more on anaerobic training methods, such as interval sprint training, which alternates intervals of high-intensity sprinting (85-100 percent; 30 seconds to 2 minutes) with intervals of rest or slow, recovery-paced running (at 43-45 percent of maximum effort for 2-15 minutes) three to four times per week.

It's important to remember that athletes involved in activities with a low aerobic component may actually see a decrease in power and strength with excessive aerobic training. These athletes should confine their aerobic training to the off-season, and only minimal aerobic training should be done during the competitive season to maintain good fitness and body composition.

Depending on your cross-training goals, you might want to direct your program to your upper body, lower body, or a combination of both. An upper body aerobics program may be beneficial for athletes such as kayakers, rowers, and tennis players. A simple upper body program might consist of alternating arm ergometer, Versa Climber, and rowing machine workouts three times a week. It's important to note that when using forms of arm exercise such as rowing or arm ergometry, your maximum heart rate is approximately 10 to 13 beats lower than when you are running; the reason being that relatively smaller muscle mass is being activated. When using your target heart rate formula for these exercises, it is important to subtract this difference from your maximum heart rate. For example, a 20-year-old would have a maximum heart rate of 187 (220 - 20 - 13) rather than 200 (220 - 20).

Tennis, basketball, or soccer players might want to focus their aerobic programs on the lower body. A program that alternates the use of exercise bike, StairMaster, or water running will contain exercises specific to the muscle groups used in these activities.

You may also choose a program that combines both upper and lower body exercises for a whole-body aerobic emphasis. This kind of program—alternating, for example, the cross-country ski machine, rowing machine, and Versa Climber three times a week—could be used by wrestlers, gymnasts, boxers, swimmers, and other aerobic athletes.

Each sport chapter in the second part of this book contains an aerobic/ anaerobic training emphasis table that is based on an approximation of the energy demands of the sport. Although these provide only rough estimates, they should help you in determining the aerobic/anaerobic emphasis your primary-sport training and cross-training should take. Each chapter also contains sample three-, five-, and seven-day aerobic/anaerobic training programs using recommended cross-training activities. For more on using the cross-training matrices in these chapters and the specifics of developing an aerobic/anaerobic endurance cross-training program, see chapter 5.

c h a p t e r

3

Cross-Training for Strength, Speed, and Power

The greatest change in sports performance in the last 25 years has been in the size, strength, and body composition of the competitor. Today's athletes are bigger; stronger; faster; and, for the most part, leaner than their predecessors. In this chapter, we'll tell you how to increase your strength, speed, and power and how to increase your size or strength with little if any increase in overall body weight. Increasing the volume and intensity of your training will likely result in a lower percentage of body fat. Before we examine how this is accomplished, let's first define some terms.

ELEMENTS OF STRENGTH TRAINING

To get the most from your cross-training, it's important to understand the differences between the terms *strength, muscular endurance, power, speed,* and *muscle balance.* As you read, think about the requirements of your sport or specific needs and also your strengths and weaknesses in that sport. Most people tend to work on their strengths, as this is easier and more self-satisfying. It's fun to work on what we do best! Working harder on your weaknesses, however, usually produces the greatest overall improvements.

Strength

Strength is the ability of a muscle to produce a maximum amount of force. It is measured by the ability to perform one repetition of an exercise at maximum resistance (1 RM). An example of maximum strength would be the greatest amount of weight one can lift in the bench press exercise.

Strength has major significance in many sports and sport skills. It is a significant factor in one's ability to put the shot, throw the javelin, create a high-velocity tennis serve, throw a fastball, and many other sport skills. Strength is also important in sport skills that require applying a large amount of force to an opponent such as in wrestling and football.

Muscular Endurance

Muscular endurance is the ability of a muscle to maintain a continuous contraction or repeated contractions over a period of time. It is measured by the number of repetitions of the movement or skill. For instance, if a person can perform 35 push-ups, then push-ups are an endurance skill for that person. If, however, a person can only do one push-up, then for him, the push-up is a strength skill. Sports requiring muscular endurance include rowing, wrestling, hurdling, sprinting, sprint swimming, and sprint cycling.

An athlete can continue to produce muscular force for only a short period of time before the energy stored in the muscle is depleted. In movements that require maximum force (strength), this occurs very quickly (after one or two repetitions). If less force is required (less than maximal), then the movement can continue for a longer period (endurance), allowing for many more repetitions.

Power

Power is the ability of the muscles to produce high levels of force in a short period of time (explosive strength). Power can be increased by strength training and is basic to a number of competitive sports. Coordination and agility are also important, especially if the execution of power is in a particular sport skill such as rebounding in basketball or a lateral movement by a football lineman.

Speed

Speed is the ability to perform a particular movement very rapidly. It is a function of distance and time. As almost any coach will tell you, the fastest way to improve speed is to improve your skill. As your coordination and efficiency in a sport movement improves, your speed increases. If you watch a beginning class in

Jean Driscoll

As a nine-time marathon champion, two-time Olympic medalist and World Record holder ,Jean Driscoll sees cross-training as one of the keys to her success. She describes her cross-training like a seasoned training partner, one that "keeps me motivated to train, particularly after a long, pressure-packed racing season."

In almost a decade of training Driscoll has enjoyed wheel-chair racing on both the road and the track, in events ranging from the 800m sprints right up to the marathon. One of the secrets to her international success has been to include wheelchair basketball, hand cycling, off-road wheelchair training and upper-body ergometers to add variety to her workouts. "Training should be an enjoyable activity that you look forward to. You have to want to come back for more."

For Driscoll, "coming back for more" allows her to constantly improve the muscular endurance which is so vital to success over all her racing distances. She focuses her cross-training on low-impact workouts, allowing her to rest race-specific muscles while maintaining aerobic fitness. "During the off season, I do as much as I can. As the racing season approaches, I concentrate on a few specific cross-training exercises that supplement my racing."

For athletes in any sport, Driscoll says, "Have fun and be imaginative. Thirst for knowledge; don't just be comfortable with what you now know. You can never learn too much about your response to training."

tennis, soccer, or martial arts, you can readily observe that speed follows mastery of the skill. There comes a time, however, after the skill is well learned that simply practicing and refining the skill no longer yields increases in speed. At this point, increasing the strength of the muscles primary to the sport movement, coupled with the continued practice of the skill, can result in increased speed.

It is no coincidence that 100-meter runners are impressively strong men and women. It is also true that many strong individuals are not fast in the 100-meter run. The key element is that as strength is gained, the skill must be continuously practiced and refined to incorporate the higher force into a smooth-skilled movement.

Muscle Balance

Muscle balance is the harmonious working of muscles that produce appropriate joint movement. Differences in strength or range of motion can result in injuries to weaker muscle groups. For example, strong quadriceps paired with weak hamstrings may result in injury during high-intensity movement.

WEIGHT TRAINING GOALS

The muscle system is the foundation of all physical exercise. No matter what activity you participate in, your muscle strength and endurance will significantly affect your exercise limits. It is also important to recognize that your muscles are not independent from the rest of the body systems and that conditioning is not limited to the muscles. Your muscles' ability to do work is dependent upon the efficiency of the heart, blood vessels, and lungs in providing energy and elimi-

Weight training goals for rowers should focus on muscular endurance.

nating waste products. Muscles, the heart, blood vessels, and the lungs are simultaneously conditioned because of their interdependence.

Weight training goals may be directed toward increases in strength and power, muscular endurance, or a combination of strength and endurance. Strength and power training is important for power lifters, weight lifters, football linemen, and weight throwers in field events. Muscular endurance training is vital to increase the aerobic capacity of the muscles for activities such as cycling, swimming, and rowing. General conditioning exercises that aim to increase both muscle strength and endurance are vital for success in sports from volleyball to gymnastics. In addition, general conditioning prepares the muscle system to meet everyday demands of all individuals, from lifting toddlers or heavy groceries, to doing yard work, climbing up stairs, and so on. Beyond these three important goals, a large number of individuals participate in weight training programs to increase the size and strength of their muscles simply because it makes them look and feel great! Regardless of your goals, a weight training program should incorporate the basic principles outlined in this chapter to maximize strength and endurance gains in an efficient and safe manner.

Training is stress and what we try to do while training is to apply stress in the correct amount with the correct frequency to achieve the maximum result. For a training effect to occur, body systems have to be overloaded or stressed. If you apply too much stress or apply the stress too frequently with insufficient rest, then improvement will not be maximized. Improvement may even be hampered and detraining (loss of gains) and injury can occur.

TYPES OF WEIGHT TRAINING EXERCISES

As a general rule, a muscle worked close to its maximum capacity will increase in strength. There is a wide variety of weight lifting equipment from which you can choose: free weights, rubber cords, isokinetic devices, pulleys, etc. Strength improvement is governed primarily by the intensity of the overload on the muscle and not the particular method of resistance, although certain methods may be more appropriate in some circumstances. The most widely used techniques for increasing strength and endurance in muscles are isotonic, eccentric, isometric, and isokinetic exercises. Table 3.1 lists the advantages and disadvantages of each.

Table 3.1   How Resistance Exercises Measure Up

Isotonic exercise

Advantages

1. Produces strength gains throughout the full range of movement.
2. Progress in strength gains is easy to evaluate because of numbered free weights and universal stacks.
3. Strength exercises can be developed to duplicate a variety of sport skills.
4. If free weights are used, balance and symmetry are enhanced.

Disadvantages

1. Equipment is cumbersome.
2. Produces more muscle soreness and greater risk of injury.
3. Most strength gains occur at the weakest point of the movement and are not uniform throughout.

Eccentric loading

Advantages

1. As effective in strength gains as isotonic and isometric exercises.
2. Increases motivation of some individuals who enjoy lifting heavier resistance.
3. May increase one's skill by lowering resistance slowly.
4. Can duplicate a variety of movement.

Disadvantages

1. Greater post-exercise soreness than other methods.
2. Partner as spotter needed to lift heavier resistance.

Isometric exercise

Advantages

1. Little time is required for training.
2. Expensive and cumbersome equipment is not needed.
3. Exercise can be performed anywhere—in home or office or while on vacation.

Disadvantages

1. Strength gains are not produced throughout the full range of movement.
2. Strength gains are difficult to evaluate; that is, no numbered weights or gauges generally are used.
3. Increases the pressure in the chest cavity, causing reduced blood flow to the heart, lungs, and brain.
4. Not as efficient in producing strength gains as isotonic and isokinetic methods.
5. Not effective in producing increases in skilled movements.
6. Motivation is difficult to maintain.
7. Muscular endurance may decrease.

Isokinetic Exercise

Advantages

1. Produces maximum resistance through the full range of movement.
2. Increases strength throughout the full range of movement.
3. Results in less injury and soreness than isometric and isotonic exercise.
4. Uniqueness of the equipment may increase motivation.
5. Strength gains are easy to determine.
6. Adaptable to specific movements patterns.
7. Permits skill improvement.

Disadvantages

1. Equipment is very expensive, with limited availability.
2. Research is still incomplete with regard to motor patterns and force/velocity relationships.
3. Applicability to sport-specific ballistic skills may be limited; may be best for tension skills (e.g., swimming and running).

Reprinted from Wathen and Roll 1994.

Isotonic Exercise

Isotonic exercise is exercise that is performed against resistance, while the load remains constant, for example, lifting free weights (i.e., barbells or weight stacks, such as those used in the universal gym). With isotonic exercise, the resistance varies with the angle of the joint. Free weights are most popular among today's athletes because the exercises can be developed to duplicate movements that are similar to sport skill movements. Resistance cords in the form of elastic bands or attached to weights or strain gauges are popular as well.

Eccentric Loading

Eccentric loading, a form of isotonic exercise, is sometimes referred to as a *negative contraction* because the muscle lengthens as it develops tension. An example would be letting yourself down slowly from a chin-up. This type of exercise tends to produce more muscle soreness than other techniques, possibly due to microtears in the muscle fibers and tendons. It is not superior to other isotonic methods but is used mainly as a supplement to other training techniques.

Isometric Exercise

An isometric exercise is a contraction performed against a fixed or immovable resistance, where tension is developed in the muscle, but there is no change in the length of the muscle or the angle of the joint. This also is referred to as a *static contraction*. An example would be holding a heavy weight in one position for a fixed amount of time or pushing against a wall.

It appears that with isometric exercise, strength development is specific only to the joint angle stimulated during training. As a result, isometric exercise does not increase strength throughout the range of movement. Isometric exercise also may inhibit the ability of the muscle to exert force rapidly, such as is necessary in the shot put and discus events. In addition, isometric exercise increases pressure in the chest cavity, which results in reduced blood flow to the heart, lungs, and brain, along with increased blood pressure. Consequently, isometric exercises are not recommended for individuals with cardiovascular problems. There also may be some decrease in muscular endurance as isometrics restrict peripheral blood flow to the muscles during the static contraction.

Isokinetic Exercise

An isokinetic exercise is an activity in which the muscle contracts maximally at a constant speed over a full range of the joint movement against a variable resistance. Isokinetic means equal motion, which is interpreted to mean equal rate of motion or equal speed. An isokinetic contraction can only be accomplished with the use of special equipment, such as a minigym that uses *accommodating resistance*. In other words, the harder you pull, the harder the minigym resists you—the resistance is always equal to the applied force. Because the resistance of the machine cannot be accelerated and any force applied against the machine results in equal reaction of force, velocity of movement is controlled.

Isokinetic exercise has become popular because it provides a speed-specific indication of the absolute strength of the muscle group being trained, thus enabling one to more closely replicate specific athletic skills. The most effective strength gains have come from slower training speeds of approximately 60 degrees (measure of distance) per second or less. Recent research, however, has indicated that training at fast speeds of movement (60-300 degrees at one second) generally increases strength at all speeds of movement. Training at fast speeds tends to increase strength at and below the exercise velocity. Exercise at lower speeds tends to produce strength increases specific to training speed.

Table 3.2 presents recommended muscle strength and endurance programs using isotonic, isometric, and isokinetic exercises for beginners and those who wish to focus in particular on strenth, endurance, or both.

Table 3.2   Strength and Endurance Training Guidelines

Isotonic (Eccentric) exercise

Frequency: 3 to 5 days a week

Duration: 6 weeks minimum

Rest: 1 to 2 minutes between sets

	Intensity	Repetitions	Sets
Beginners	10 RM*	10	3 per exercise
Strength	2-6 RM	2-6	3 per exercise
Endurance	15-25 RM	15-25	3 per exercise
Combination	8-12 RM	8-12	3 per exercise

*RM (Repetition Maximum): The amount of weight that you can successfully lift through the full range of movement before you fatigue. 10 RM is the amount you can lift 10 times before fatiguing.

Isometric exercise

Frequency: 3 to 5 days a week

Duration: 6 weeks minimum

Intensity: Maximum force held for 5 to 7 seconds

Repetitions: 5 to 10

Isokinetic exercise

Frequency: 3 to 4 days a week

Duration: 6 weeks

Intensity: Maximum

Repetitions: 8 to 15 (3 sets for each muscle group)

Speed: 60 to 300 degrees per second. The exercise should be similar to the sport skill being trained. The training speed should be as fast or faster than the speed involved in the actual athletic event.

Reprinted from Wathan 1994.

DEVELOPING A WEIGHT TRAINING PROGRAM

Before starting your exercise program, remember the three basic principles introduced in chapter 2: intensity (the degree of overload or stressfulness of the exercise), duration (the amount of time utilized for each exercise session), and frequency (the number of exercise sessions per week). As in aerobic and anaerobic training, generally the more intense, the longer, and more frequent the weight training program, the greater the benefits. Intensity and duration are interrelated, with the total amount of work accomplished being the important factor.

Generally, to increase muscle strength, the intensity of effort should be near maximum with a low number of repetitions; and to gain muscle endurance, the intensity of effort should be lower with a high number of repetitions.

The intensity level for strength gains is believed to be between one and six repetitions maximum (RM). One RM is the maximum load that you can lift successfully one time through the full range of movement, two RM is the amount you can lift successfully two times through the full range of movement, and so on. Weight training research indicates that weight loads exceeding 75 percent of maximum are necessary for promoting strength gains because the most important factor in strength development is intensity. Ten RM weight load usually corresponds to about 75 percent of that maximum.

There is no ideal number of repetitions for endurance gains. The program should be specific to the sport. For example, if you are involved in long crew races, repetitions of 150 are not uncommon. Conversely, crew racers may utilize 50 repetitions in their training programs. However, for an average person, performing anywhere between 15 and 25 repetitions is appropriate for endurance gains.

Selecting the Amount of Weight

An important factor in beginning your program is selection of the appropriate weight to be lifted. The key is to select the amount of weight that allows you to perform the right number of repetitions for your program. For example, in a general sport training program that focuses evenly on building both strength and muscular endurance, we recommend that you perform three sets of the following repetitions:

Set 1 - 10 repetitions
Set 2 - 10 repetitions
Set 3 - 10 repetitions

You should choose a weight for set 1 that you can lift 10 times (10 repetitions). You should work hard to perform the tenth repetition. If you could have done more than 10 repetitions, then the weight was too light. If you were only able to do six, eight, or nine repetitions, then the weight was too heavy. The first few weight lifting sessions will be primarily testing sessions to determine the proper weight that you should lift. It is important that you keep accurate records.

After your first set of 10 repetitions, you should rest from one to two minutes before your second set. You may find that on your second set you are able to perform 12 repetitions of the same weight you used for the first set. If this occurs, you will need to add weight for the second set to bring your repetitions down to 10. The same may occur with your third set. This increase in strength with successive sets often occurs and is a result of the influx of blood and increased nerve stimulation to the muscle, making it better able to respond to the demands you make on it. Be sure to rest one to two minutes between all three sets.

A sample general program with increasing weight might look like this:

Set 1	10 repetitions	x amount of weight
Set 2	10 repetitions	x plus 5 pounds
Set 3	10 repetitions	x plus 10 pounds

Again, note that the key to the program is the number of repetitions. If, after 10 weeks, you want to focus your sport training program mainly on strength development, then you might do three sets of eight repetitions or a progressive program as follows:

Set 1	8 repetitions	x amount of weight
Set 2	8 repetitions	x plus 10 pounds
Set 3	8 repetitions	x plus 15 pounds

Conversely, if, after 10 weeks of a sport conditioning program, you wanted to shade your program toward endurance development, you might choose the following type of program:

Set 1	10 repetitions	x amount of weight
Set 2	12 repetitions	x amount of weight
Set 3	12 repetitions	x plus 5 pounds

After you have followed the general sport training program for 8 to 10 weeks, your skeletal-muscular and cardiorespiratory systems will be in better condition to shift toward a strength or endurance program if you so desire.

Remember! The number of repetitions and the appropriate amount of weight, not how hard you work, determine whether you are performing a general, strength, or endurance program. How hard you work will determine your level of success and the amount of gain you achieve. We assume you are willing to work hard, or you would not be reading this book!

Remember the continuum:

Strength development	2-6 repetitions
General sport training	8-12 repetitions
Endurance development	15-25 repetitions

How Often Should You Lift?

The general rule for weight lifting is to exercise the various muscle groups three times per week. Just as in a running or bicycling program, the best results are achieved when stress is applied in a hard day/easy day fashion. This approach allows for cellular changes to occur at an optimum rate and avoids overstressing or overtraining. In weight training, we follow the hard/easy system by working hard one day and then following it with a day off. So a three-day-a-week program would follow a M-W-F or T-Th-Sat routing. The off-days allow the muscles time to recover from the stress that lifting imposes upon them.

Many experienced weight lifters lift more than three times per week (i.e., six days per week), but they will exercise a body part only three times per week. In this program, the lifter would work his chest, back, and shoulders on M-W-F and his legs and arms on T-Th-Sat. This way each body part is exercised three times per week with a day off in between. This program is called a split-routine and is performed primarily by advanced lifters who perform multiple sets of multiple exercises for a specific body part. Examples of these exercises include the regular bench press, inclined bench press, and declined bench press for chest development.

In summary, you should work each body part three times per week. You can do so in a routine in which you do all of your desired exercises three times per week, or a split routine in which you perform a portion of your exercises three times per week and the remaining portion on the alternate days. For the beginning lifter, we recommend exercising three times per week as it is mentally easier to gear yourself up to three workouts per week than six sessions per week.

How Many Sets?

Research in the area of weight training and strength development has found that three to five sets of an exercise produce the most gains. You will experience gains with one set

Varying the number of repetitions and amount of weight allows you to focus on the kind of training you want to emphasize: power or endurance.

and even greater gains with two and three sets. After three sets, there is a leveling off of the gains. Performing four or five sets of an exercise produces more gains than three sets, but the amount of this increase is less than occurs during the first three sets. In other words, you have to work harder for fewer results after three sets than you do for the first three sets. The law of diminishing returns prevails. One recommendation is that you perform three sets of your major exercises. After you are conditioned to the exercises and want greater results, then you can go up to five sets. After five sets the curve flattens out, and little is gained for your efforts.

Overload and Progressive Resistance

Muscle strength only develops when muscles are *overloaded*—forced to contract at maximum or near maximum tension. Muscle contractions at these tension levels produce physiological changes in the muscles, resulting in strength gains. If muscles are not overloaded to this degree, they do not increase in strength or in size (hypertrophy). Muscles adapt only to the load to which they are subjected.

A maximum overload results in maximum strength gains, whereas a minimum overload produces only minimum strength gains.

Also, you must progressively increase the weight being lifted to ensure future strength gains. If the intensity of the training load is not increased, only existing strength levels are maintained. With progressive overload the muscle responds with an increase in size and strength. The same overload response can be used to increase muscular endurance by progressively increasing the number of repetitions performed or the amount of resistance used. If training stops, the lack of stimulus will result in a loss of muscle size (atrophy) and strength.

Exercise Specificity

The demands of the exercise must be sufficient to force muscles to adapt; subsequent muscle adaptations will be specific to the type of training performance. This concept is known as *specificity*. For example, aerobic activity develops aerobic capacity, and anaerobic activity develops anaerobic capacity.

Research indicates that muscle adaptations are specific to the type of training performed because exercise not only affects muscles but also nerve control of muscles. The nerve pathways appear to become more efficient with continued exercise. The efficiency, however, is specific only to the particular exercise. Research also indicates that the joint angle of exercise, the type of exercise (isotonic, isometric, or isokinetic), and the speed and range of movement all produce a variety of specific muscle adaptations.

It is important that you assess your strengths and weaknesses and the requirements of your sport so that you can train as specifically as possible to maximize your performance.

Lifting Speed

It is also important to maintain a consistent application of force by raising and lowering the weight in a controlled manner. This type of movement subjects the muscles to the same level of stress during both the lifting and lowering phases. Generally, the lift phase should take about one to two seconds and the lowering phase approximately two to three seconds. Fast movements require more strength at the beginning of the lift and less force during the lowering portion of the movement. High speeds of lifting and lowering are less productive in strength development with the added possibility of causing injury to muscle tissue.

Recovery and Order of Exercises

Progressive training becomes less effective when muscles become so fatigued that the individual cannot continue to lift the maximum amount of weight. Also, overloading a fatigued muscle may lead to soreness and injury. To avoid soreness and injury, follow these three simple rules for proper recovery:

1. Exercise large-muscle groups before smaller ones. Large-muscle movements are fatiguing when the small muscles involved in the movement are already exhausted. For example, when working the upper body, exercise the chest and back muscles before performing exercises that work primarily the

arms or forearm. If not, the fatigued arm muscle may be the limiting factor rather than the chest or back muscles that you are trying to exercise.

2. Arrange your strength exercises so that successive exercises only minimally affect the muscle groups that were just trained previously.

3. Allow 48 hours rest between strength workouts for physiological recovery. During this time, you may wish to cross-train for aerobic endurance or flexibility.

Combining Exercises for Muscle Balance

To promote muscle balance, flexibility, and injury-free training, opposite muscle groups known as *prime movers*, or *antagonists*, should be exercised in the same session. For example, one should complement a quadriceps exercise (leg extension) with a hamstring exercise (leg curl [flexion]) and chest work (pectoral presses) with back work (rhomboid squeezes [rows]) during the same workout. This approach ensures balance and harmony of muscle groups that work together in a movement.

A javelin thrower uses his chest and anterior (front) shoulder muscles to throw the javelin and also must use the upper back and posterior (back) shoulder muscles to slow the arm down after the javelin is released. If he develops the chest muscles alone, then he runs the risk of strength imbalance and injury to his back. The typical combinations of prime movers and antagonists are as follows:

Chest/back   Abdominals/lower back
Shoulders/lats   Gastrocnemius/soleus
Biceps/triceps   Anterior tibialis/posterior tibialis
Quadriceps/hamstrings

PLYOMETRICS

Plyometrics are exercises in which muscles are loaded suddenly and forced to stretch before the contraction for movement occurs. The greater the stretch put on the muscle from its resting length immediately before the concentric (or shortening) contraction, the greater the resistance the muscle can overcome. Plyometrics emphasize the speed of the eccentric (or lengthening) contraction phase. The rate of stretch is more critical than the magnitude of stretch.

Plyometrics exercises were developed to enable the muscle to reach maximum strength in as short a time as possible. An example includes jumping off a box onto the ground and rebounding as quickly as possible. The deceleration and acceleration of body weight provides the overload. Upper body plyometrics include medicine ball throws and catches and quick types of push-ups. Plyometric exercises are beneficial in sports, such as volleyball, downhill skiing, and jumping events, that require the application of maximal force during high-speed movements, sometimes referred to as speed/strength. An athlete should be well conditioned to a strength training program before attempting plyometrics. Refer to table 3.3 for plyometric intensity levels.

Plyometric exercises emphasize speed and force to train muscles used in sports involving high-speed movements.

Here are some plyometric terms and activities:

Jump: a movement that concludes with a landing on two feet

Jump in place: vertical jump performed in place (tuck, pike, split squat, squat, power jumps)

Standing jump: a maximal jump that may be linear, vertical, or lateral

Hop: a move that starts and concludes with a single foot landing using either the same or alternating feet (short hop, 10 repetitions; long hop, 30 repetitions or more)

Bound: a series of movements in which one lands successfully on alternate feet (short-respond bound, 25-30 meters; long-respond bound, 60 meters or more)

Caution: The combination of high force and speed produces significant loads on the muscles, tendons, and ligaments. These structures need to be well-conditioned to both force and speed before plyometric exercises are attempted. Proper technique and form are very important in performing these exercises in order to reduce the impact shock and protect the joints and joint structure.

Table 3.3   Plyometric Drills Classified by Intensity Level

	Low intensity	Medium intensity	High intensity	Shock
In-place jumps	Squat jump Split squat jump Cycled split squat jump (also, ankle bounce, ice skater, lateral cone jump)	Pike jump Double-leg tuck jump (also, jump up, lateral hop)	Double-leg vertical power jump Single-leg vertical power jump Single-leg tuck jump	
Standing jumps		Standing triple jump (also, standing long-jump)		
Short-response hops		Double- and single-leg zigzag hop and double-leg hop Double-leg hop	Single-leg hop and double- and single-leg speed hop Single-leg hop and double- and single-leg speed hop	
Long-response hops		Double-leg hop	Single-leg hop and double- and single-leg speed hop	
Short-response bounds		Alternate leg bound Combination bound		
Long-response bounds		Alternate leg bound Combination bound		
Shocks				In-depth jump Box jump Drop-and-catch push-up
Upper body plyometrics	Medicine ball sit-up Plyometric sit-up (also, two-hand, overhead forward throw; clap push-ups)	Medicine ball push-up (also, overhead backward throw, underhand forward throw, Russian twist)		

Reprinted from Allerheiligen 1994.

WEIGHT TRAINING EXERCISES

This section provides a selection of the most effective and popular exercises for various body parts. These include exercises with free weights and machines. The section includes weight training exercises for chest, back, shoulders, arms, (biceps, triceps, and forearms), trunk (abdominal and lower back), hips, thighs, and calves.

Bench Press

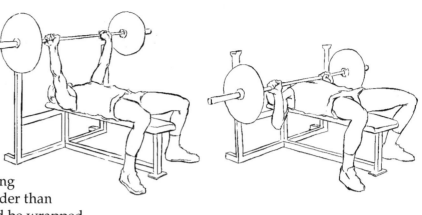

Muscles used:
Primary: Pectoralis major
Additional: Anterior Deltoid,
 Biceps Brachii, Triceps Brachii
Technique:
The weight is lowered to the
 chest and returned to the starting
 position. Hands are slightly wider than
 shoulder width; thumbs should be wrapped
 around the bar, with feet flat on the floor.

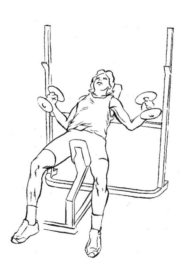

Inclined Dumbbell Fly

Muscles used:
Same as bench press, with more
 emphasis on the upper Pectoralis
 Major fibers
Technique:
Lower the dumbbells to the side with
 a wide elbow position, then return
 to the starting position.

Declined Bench Press

Muscles used:
Primary: Same as bench press,
 but with more emphasis on
 lower portion of the
 Pectoralis Major
Technique:
The weight is lowered to the chest and returned to the starting position. Hands are
 slightly wider than shoulder width; thumbs
 should be wrapped around the bar, with
 feet flat on the floor.

Pec Deck Machine

Muscles used:
Pectoralis Major with emphasis on the inner/
medial fibers

Technique:
From the starting position bring your arms
together until the machine arms nearly
touch, then return to the starting position.

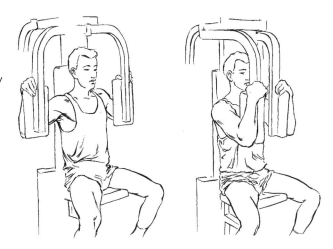

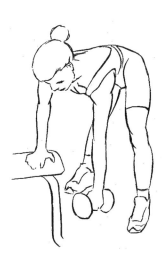
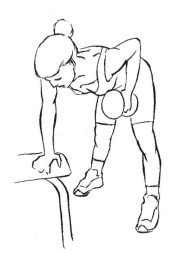

One-Arm Dumbbell Rowing

Muscles used:
Rhomboids, *Teres* Group, and Latissimus
Dorsi

Technique:
Place dumbbell on floor in front of bench.
Put left leg back, knee straight but not
locked. Bend right knee slightly. Bend
over and hold dumbbell with left hand,
palm in, about 6" off floor. Put right
hand on the bench, elbow straight. Pull
dumbbell straight up to the side of your
chest, keeping your arm close to your
side. Return to starting position using
the same path. Inhale up; exhale down.
Reverse position and repeat movement
on the right side.

Seated Pulley Rows

Muscles used:
Same muscles as dumbbell rowing

Technique:
Knees are bent and the back is held
straight. The hand grip is brought
to the chest and then returned to the
starting position.

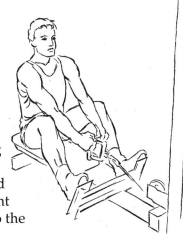

Lateral Pull Down

Muscles used:
Latissimus Dorsi
Technique:
A wide grip is taken on the bar and then the bar is pulled to shoulder level. For heavy resistance, a seated position can be used to enable a restraining bar to be placed above the knees in order to keep the body down.

Military Press

Muscles used:
Primary: Trapezius, Deltoid
Additional: Supraspinatus, Levator Scapulae
Technique:
Feet are placed flat on the floor approximately shoulder-width apart. The hand grip is slightly wider than shoulder width. The bar is pressed overhead and then returned to the starting position. A weight rack can be used to provide a safety measure for heavy weights. When lifting high resistances in this lift, a weight belt may be used to support the lower back.

Upright Rowing

Muscles used:
Primary: Trapezius, Deltoid
Additional: Supraspinatus, Levator Scapulae
Technique:
A close, narrow grip is used. The bar is brought up to just below chin level and returned to the starting position. Elbows should remain even with or slightly below shoulder line.

Shoulder Dips

Muscles used:

Primary: Anterior Deltoid, Pectoralis Major

Additional: Triceps Brachii, Biceps Brachii

Technique:

This exercise is performed on parallel bars. From the upright position, lower yourself to as low a position as possible, then push up to the upright position. The exercise may be performed with weights held between the ankles (figure c).

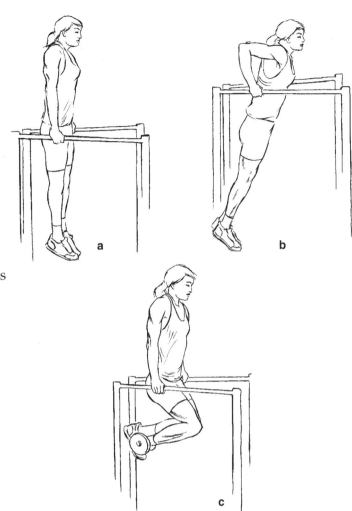

Bicep Curl

Muscles used:

Primary: Biceps Brachii, Brachialis

Additional: Coracobrachialis, Brachioradialis, Anterior Deltoid

Technique:

Feet and hands shoulder-width apart. The bar is brought up to the shoulders and returned to the starting position. Keep your back straight and knees slightly bent to discourage cheating. Concentrate on lifting with your biceps, not your back.

Seated Dumbbell Curls

Muscles used:
Same as bicep curl
Technique:
Seated position with feet and
    knees wide apart. The elbow
    of the lifting arm is in tight to
    the thigh. The opposite hand
    rests on the opposite thigh.
    After the target number of
    repetitions is achieved, the
    weight is switched to the other hand.

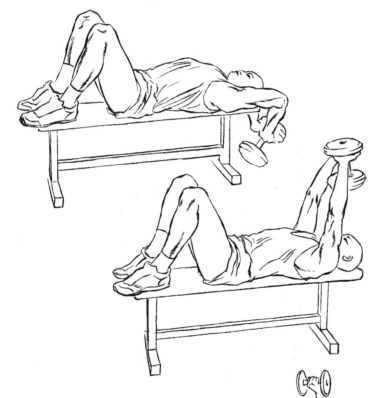

Tricep Pullovers

Muscles used:
Primary: Triceps Brachii
Additional: Pectoralis Major,
    Latissimus Dorsi
This exercise is especially
    effective for working the
    long head of the Triceps.
Technique:
Lie on a bench with your feet
    on the bench or flat on the
    floor. Hold the dumbbell with
    both hands and bring it up from
    the floor to a position directly
    above the head. Return it to near
    the floor.

Seated Tricep Dumbbell Curls

Muscles used:
Primary: Triceps Brachii
Additional: Deltoid
Technique:
From a seated position, using
    one arm at a time, bring the
    dumbbell down to a position
    between the shoulder blades
    (scapulae) and return to the
    starting position.

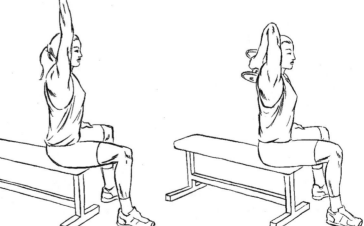

Tricep Pulldowns

Muscles used:
Primary: Triceps Brachii
Additional: Posterior Deltoid, Latissimus Dorsi
Technique:
Use a narrow grip. Bring the bar down close to the body to a position in front of the hips with the arms fully extended. Caution against the use of the trunk in an effort to handle more weight.

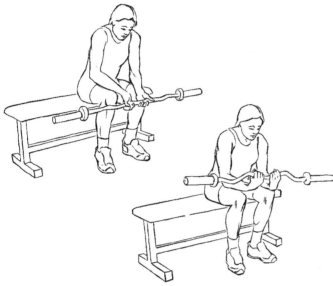

Forearm Curls

Muscles used:
Primary: Forearm Flexors, Flexor Carpi Radialis, Flexor Carpi Ulnaris
Additional: Flexor Digitorum Profundus, Flexor Digitorum Superficialis
Technique:
Rest the forearms on the thighs for support. Hold the bar with a palm-up grip, and flex the hands and wrists upwards. A reverse, palm-down grip can be used to perform a reversed forearm curl for development of the posterior forearm muscles.

Bent-Knee Sit-Ups

Muscles used:
Primary: Rectus Abdominus
Additional: Internal Obliques, External Obliques, Transverse Abdominus
Technique:
Start flat on the floor with feet secured under a dresser, pads, or sit-up board. A spotter can also hold your feet. Bend knees to at least a 90-degree angle to place less stress on the lower back. Straight-up sit-ups work primarily the rectus abdominus while twisting sit-ups (twisting at waist with hand behind head) add work for the oblique muscles.

Crunches

Muscles used:
Same as bent-knee sit-ups
Technique:
Place legs on a bench, ankles crossed. Start this sit-up flat on the floor and bring torso up until elbows touch the knees. Do not lift with your neck.

Alternate Knee-Touching Sit-Ups

Muscles used:
Abdominal Group
Technique:
Starting flat on the floor, raise torso and leg upward and touch your elbow to your opposite knee, being careful not to pull on the neck. Repeat for the opposite elbow and knee. This exercise is excellent for oblique development.

Incline Bench Sit-Ups

Muscles used:
Abdominal Group
Technique:
Start flat on the bench and move to a fully upright position. The use of weights adds resistance for greater strength development.

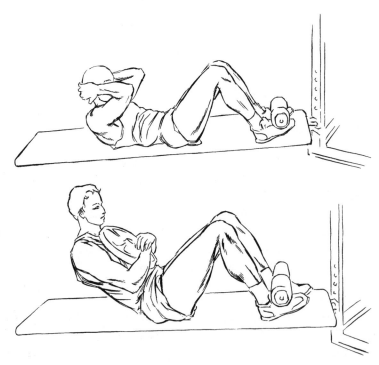

Side Bend with Dumbbell

Muscles used:
Primary: Transverse Abdominus
Additional: Internal Obliques, External Obliques

Technique:
From an upright standing position, bend to the side, stretching the opposite side. Be sure not to lock your knees and to keep your abdominals fully contracted. Try to concentrate on isolating the musculature to slowly return to the upright position. Be careful not to use too heavy a weight as this area will increase in size.

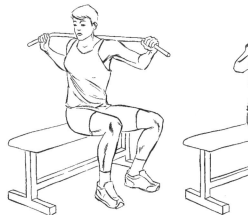

Bar Twists

Muscles used:
Primary: Transverse Abdominus
Additional: Internal Oblique, External Oblique

Technique:
From a seated or standing position with a bar or broomstick on your shoulders and your hands spread wide and grasping the bar, twist to one side and reverse twist to the other. Try to isolate the abdominal muscles while performing this exercise.

Back Hyperextension

Muscles used:
Primary: Erector Spinae

Technique:
Using a back hyperextension machine, start from the down (flexed) position and move upward into a hyperextended position. This exercise can be performed with light weights to build greater strength (figure c). Take care, however, as the lower back muscles are subject to spasms. Use only light weights.

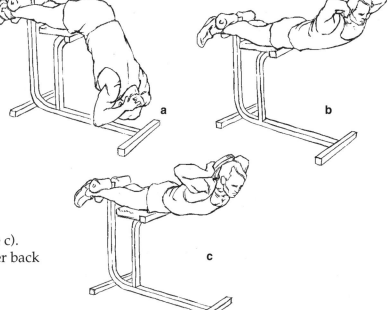

Squats

Muscles used:

Primary: Gluteals, Quadriceps, Hamstrings

Full squats involve more Gluteal use.

Technique:

The safest way to perform squats is to use a squat rack, as shown in figures a, b, and c. Starting from an upright position with the bar on your shoulders, bend at the knees and slightly lower yourself to a position of a 90-degree angle between your thigh and leg. This is a half squat. In the full squat, lower yourself to a fully lowered position. Full squats (figure c) put great stress on the knees and can produce injuries in susceptible individuals. Take special care while doing full squats. We recommend half squats over full squats.

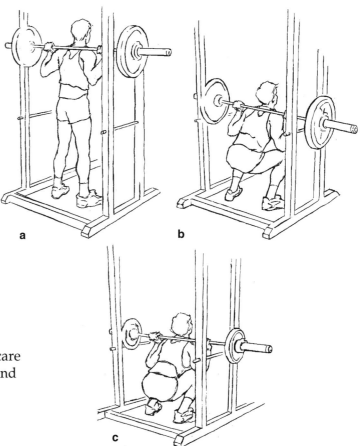

a   b

c

Leg Press

Muscles used:

Primary: Quadriceps

Additional: Hamstrings, Gluteals

Technique:

Adjust the seat so that there is a 90-degree angle or less at the knees. From this position, press until legs are extended and then return to the starting position.

FOUR-WAY HIP EXERCISES

1. Hip Flexion

Muscles used:
Primary: Illiopsoas
Additional: Rectus Femoris, Quadriceps
Technique:
Face away from the weight pulley. Starting with your leg behind you, bring the leg forward.

2. Hip Extension

Muscles used:
Primary: Gluteals
Additional: Hamstrings
Technique:
Place your leg in front of you, then bring your leg backwards into a hyperextended position behind you. Keep your support leg slightly bent at the knee.

3. Hip Adduction

Muscles used:
Primary: Adductor Group (Groin Muscles)
Technique:
Stand with legs wide apart, then bring one leg inward and across in front of the support leg.

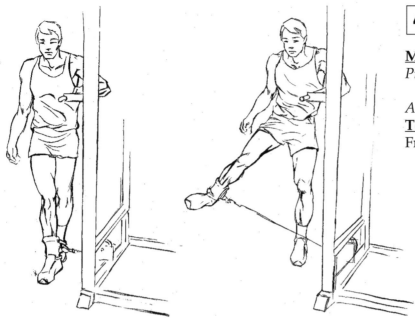

4. Hip Abduction

Muscles used:
Primary: Gluteus medius and
    maximus.
Additional: Tensor fascia latae
Technique:
From a position slightly in front
    of the support leg, move the
    leg outward to the side.

Leg Extension

Muscles used:
Quadriceps
Technique:
Move the legs from
    a flexed position to
    an extended
    position, pause
    momentarily, and
    return. Start with
    your legs at a right
    angle and pause
    with your legs
    straight.

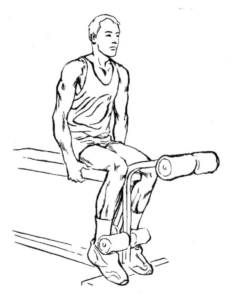

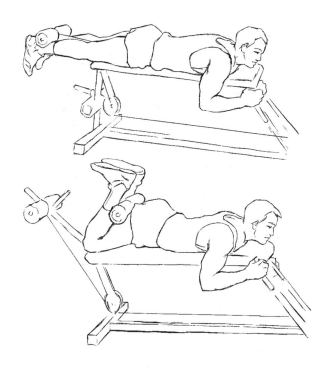

Standing Toe Raises

Muscles used:
Primary: Posterior calf (Gastrocnemius, Soleus)
Additional: Tibialis Posterior
Technique:
Starting from a position in which your heels are lower than your forefeet, press upwards using the calf muscles until you are standing on your toes.

Seated Toe Raises

Muscles used:
Same as standing toe raises
Technique:
Slide your feet halfway down the foot platform so that the balls of your feet are on the platform but your heels are off. Press forward and back from a toes-back to a toes-forward position.

Leg Flexion

Muscles used:
Primary: Hamstrings (Semitendinosus, Semimembranosus, Biceps Femoris)
Technique:
Lying prone on the bench with your heels behind the pads, flex the legs and bring your heels toward your buttocks.

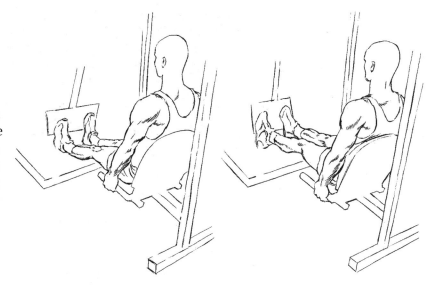

chapter

4

Cross-Training for Agility, Balance, and Flexibility

In most physical activities, the body is always experiencing changes in movement. Many of the movements that help us maintain control of our bodies in precarious or reactive situations are reflexive (or involuntary and automatic) in nature. We perform other movements voluntarily, however, because we have found such movements to be effective from previous experiences in specific situations requiring control.

Agility, balance, and flexibility are essential variables in most rigorous and competitive physical activities. Agility is the ability to change or alter quickly and accurately the direction of one's body movement during physical activity. Balance is the ability to maintain movement control throughout the execution of various movements. Both agility and balance to a large extent are dependent on neuromuscular coordination and reaction time. Agility and balance may be improved with increased flexibility and muscular strength. Flexibility is the ability to move freely through a full range of motion. We will discuss this important element in more detail later in this chapter.

Jeff Galloway

Jeff Galloway has been running since 1958 when, as an overweight high school student, he joined his high school cross-country and track teams to fullfill his high school activity requirement. He progressed to become a state high school 2-mile champion, and a collegiate All-American in cross-country and track. Jeff was a member of the U.S. Olympic track team, running the Olympic 10,000 meters in 1972 in Munich. In 1973, Jeff set an American record in the 10 mile with a time of 47:49. Jeff is equally well remembered for his marathon performances, running a personal record for 26.2 miles in 2:16 at the age of 35.

Perhaps Jeff's greatest contributions to track and road racing has been as an author, marathon coach, and fitness educator. His best-known books include, *Galloway's Book on Running, Return of the Tribes to Peachtree,* and *Marathon.* Jeff was the first winner and later a key organizer of Atlanta's Peachtree Road Race, and co-founder in 1978 of the Avon International Women's Marathon. Jeff conducts marathon programs and clinics as well as running camps and fitness vacations. Through these avenues, as well as being a contributor to *Runners World* and other publications, Jeff has become the mentor for the distance runner in the United States and throughout the world.

Jeff has been utilizing and recommending cross-training for runners since 1988 and has placed particular emphasis on water running for conditioning, improving running efficiency, and eliminating negative (patho-mechanical) motions, which are inhibited by water running. Jeff has long recommended muscle strengthening to compensate for weakness and prevent injuries. He suggests you ease into each new cross-training exercise, starting with short bouts of exercise and working up to longer sessions of up to as much as 60 minutes. He also suggests a variety of additional cross-training exercises such as the cross-country ski machine, cycling, and swimming, which may be performed alternatively or serially.

An integral component of balance, stability, is the body's resistance to losing its static equilibrium or its resistance to changing position in relationship to some support. Static stability means maintaining balance while remaining stationary for a specific period of time. The importance of possessing good static stability can be seen in starts in swimming, track, and speed skating, which require one to hold a precarious position where stability can be easily lost. To maintain this position, the athlete typically lowers her center of gravity (the pelvis) and widens her base of support. Dynamic stability refers to maintaining balance while constantly changing position. Most sport activities (e.g., wrestling, football, gymnastics, basketball, weight lifting, martial arts, throwing, etc.) require that the athlete maintains both static and dynamic stability.

The act of standing motionless (for instance, in starting positions in diving, shot put, and discus) is actually a continuous process of tiny adjustments in body positions to keep the center of gravity over the base of support. The smaller the base, the more accurate the adjustments have to be. Strong extensor muscles in your legs and ankles are essential for these kinds of activities.

Sudden movement or acceleration of body parts, on the other hand, requires the body to respond with reflex movements that aid in preventing a loss of balance. For example, in throwing, the lead foot provides a base of support for the movement.

When using cross-training activities to enhance agility and balance, try to match the movement of the activity to those required by your primary sport.

In starting and stopping movements, the center of gravity position must be low and along the line of application of the movement. The side roll in volleyball requires players to roll to the side and onto the feet, rather than landing in an uncontrolled position, which would mean more time to recover to a ready position.

Enhancing Agility and Balance

When using cross-training activities to enhance agility and balance, it's important to choose activities that closely resemble your primary sport. For example, zigzag course running and lateral movement drills resemble many of the movements required in ice hockey and basketball. You may also adapt the cross-training activity movements to the specific needs of your primary sport's starting and stopping movements. For instance, downhill skiers might use box jumping or other plyometrics to aid in strengthening their muscles for better balance. Here is a list of activities that focus on agility and balance:

Agility	*Balance*
Shuttle runs (run to a stop, then run back)	Plyometrics
Speed/agility ladder	Balance beam exercises
Lateral movement drills (moving quickly to the right, then to the left)	Ball balancing (see page 58)
	Gymnastics
Strength exercises	Strength exercises
Modern dance, ballet, aerobic dance	Sprints
Racquet sports	Gazelle jumping (see page 59)
Basketball	Inside barrel balancing (see page 59)
Gymnastics	Box and hurdle jumping (see page 58)
Martial arts	Yoga

AGILITY AND BALANCE ACTIVITIES

The following activities will help improve your agility and balance. They can be especially helpful for those in throwing and striking sports (such as baseball and volleyball) that require strong whole-body preparation, execution, and recovery skills.

Ankle Platform

Technique:
With the help of a partner or nearby support, stand on the platform with one foot and shift weight from heel to toe as in walking, then shift to the opposite foot. Arms should be held wide for maintaining balance.

Ball Balancing

Technique:
With the aid of a partner, stand on a large stability ball with feet shoulder-width apart. Maintain balance by moving feet with arms spread wide.

Box and Hurdle Jumping

Technique:
Stand on top of the lower box, feet shoulder-width apart. Jump onto the floor and, immediately upon landing, spring upwards to land with both feet on the top of the higher box.

Gazelle Jumping

Technique:

Run forward three steps and then jump as high as you can, taking off on one foot. Land on both feet. Repeat run and jump with opposite foot.

Inside Barrel Balancing

Technique:

With the aid of a partner, position your feet shoulder-width apart. Start by shifting your weight from one leg to the other in a rocking fashion using your arms for balance.

Hurdle Jumping

Technique:
With your knees flexed approximately 90 degrees, take off with both feet, bringing knees up high, clearing the hurdle, and landing on both feet. Then immediately spring over the next hurdle. *Caution:* start with a lower obstacle until you are confident you can clear the hurdle height.

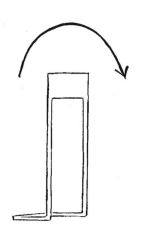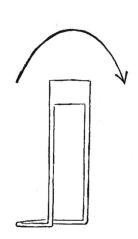

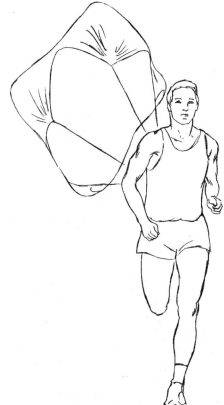

Power Fitness Chutes

Technique:
With the chute in place, face the direction of the wind and run short sprints with a rest period in between.

Speed/Agility Ladder

Technique:
Run as quickly as you can, bringing the knees up high without skipping a space between the ladder rungs.

Side-Stepping Resister

Technique:
With resister cord attached to both ankles and feet shoulder-width apart, flat on the floor, move one foot sideways against resistance cord. Repeat with the opposite leg.

Weight Kicking

Technique:
With the pulley around the right ankle and arm grasping a support bar, gradually bring leg forward in a kicking motion. Make sure there is no slack in the cord before kicking. If you experience any knee pain, discontinue the exercise. Repeat with opposite leg.

Wrist Resister

Technique:

Begin the throwing motion with your elbow
flexed approximately 90 degrees. Use the
same throwing motion that you would for a
baseball or football. Start with a very low
resistance and gradually increase.

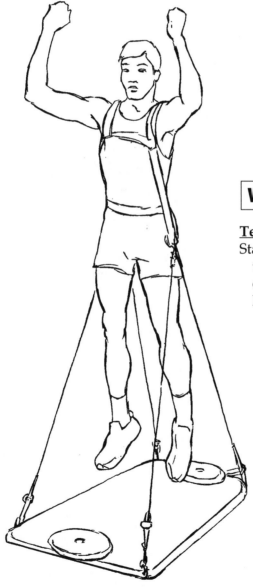

Vertical Resister

Technique:

Start with both feet shoulder-width apart on
the platform. Bend knees slightly and then
explode upward against the resistance
harness.

Jump and Sprinting Circuit

Technique:

The following illustration shows how you might put together a circuit of plyometric and sprinting agility exercises. Make sure you warm up properly, stretching and jogging 10 to 15 minutes before starting the circuit.

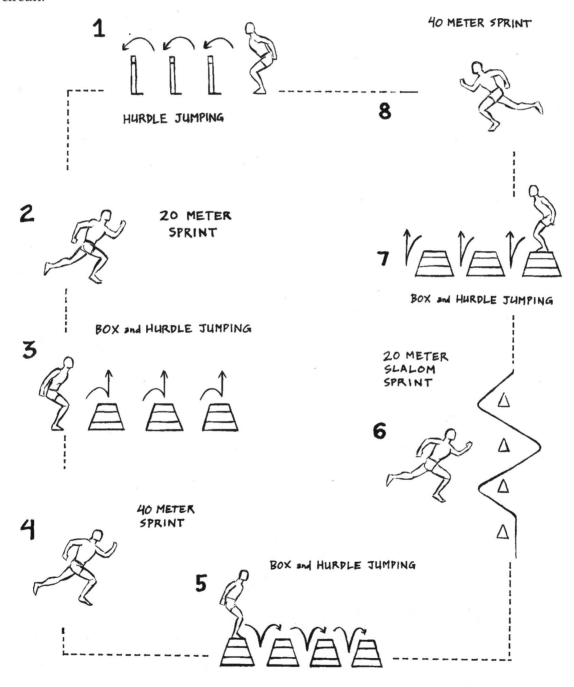

1 HURDLE JUMPING

2 20 METER SPRINT

3 BOX and HURDLE JUMPING

4 40 METER SPRINT

5 BOX and HURDLE JUMPING

6 20 METER SLALOM SPRINT

7 BOX and HURDLE JUMPING

8 40 METER SPRINT

FLEXIBILITY

As mentioned earlier, flexibility is the ability to move freely through a full, nonrestricted, and pain-free range of motion about a joint or series of joints. Flexibility plays an important part in all sport activities in that it prevents muscle joint problems; increases movement efficiency; aids in increasing balance and reducing reaction time; and reduces uncoordinated, awkward movement. Stretching exercises play a vital role in increasing flexibility by reducing joint stiffness and preventing muscle and connective tissue shortening that may occur from injury, disease, inactivity, or overtraining. Besides stretching, other activities that can help promote improved flexibility include dance, racquet sports, gymnastics, swimming, aerobic dance, martial arts, and yoga.

Types of Stretching

There are three general types of stretching: *static* stretching (holding the stretch position for a set period of time); *dynamic* or *ballistic* stretching (rapid, bouncing, or jerking movements); and *proprioceptive neuromuscular facilitation* (PNF), which involves preceding a static stretch with an isometric contraction. In PNF, a training partner moves the limb passively through its full range of motion. Near the end point of the range of motion, the muscle is isometrically contracted for 6 to 10 seconds. The muscle is then relaxed and then further stretched statically by the partner.

Dynamic stretching is not as effective as static stretching or PNF as it may lead to injury and soreness and is less effective in increasing range of movement. Rapid, dynamic (ballistic) stretching may stimulate stretch receptor mechanisms in the muscles and joints, which in turn cause the muscle fibers to contract to

Because stretching exercises play a vital role in increasing flexibility, they should be part of every athletes's workout.

protect the joint and can result in tearing of the very muscle fibers you are trying to stretch. PNF may be a little more efficient in increasing the range of motion than the static method; however, it necessitates finding a training partner.

Stretching Principles

1. No matter what the nature of exercise to come, a slow, gradual warm-up consisting of calisthenics, stretching, and slow jogging always should precede exercise even if you are highly trained.

2. Your warm-up should take at least 10 to 15 minutes.

3. Stretching should be slow and thorough and is most efficient following a warm-up of light activity like slow jogging or calisthenics.

4. Initial stretching should be gentle and specific to the muscles that will receive the most stress.

5. Jogging after stretching and before your main activity should be conducted at an intensity and rate specific to your anticipated activity and level of fitness.

6. Only a few minutes should lapse between the completion of the warm-up and your cross-training activity.

7. Be prepared to make minor adjustments to your regular stretching routine. You may be more flexible on some days than on others.

8. Experiment with different types of warm-ups to find the one that best fits your body. The warm-up should feel good.

9. A portion of the warm-up exercise should consist of a skill drill and other skilled movements, such as low-intensity strokes, throwing, kicking, and striking movements, related to the anticipated activity (a "dress rehearsal" of movements to be performed later).

10. Remember to stretch and cool down following your workout as well.

FLEXIBILITY EXERCISES

The following stretching exercises stretch the most commonly used muscles of the body, or those that will experience the most stress. Certain flexibility exercises have a greater potential for injury; therefore, caution should be observed when performing such exercises. Be sure to inhale before the stretch and exhale during the stretch. Releasing the breath decreases muscular tension allowing for a deeper, more thorough stretch. Stretching exercises should always proceed from larger muscle groups to smaller muscle groups.

Upper Chest Stretch

Muscles stretched:
Anterior shoulder, Rotators
Technique:
Stand with your
   feet slightly
   apart. Grasp your
   hands behind your back
   and raise your arms.
   Hold for 10 seconds.
   Repeat five times.

Neck Stretch

Muscles stretched:
Lateral neck
Technique:
Stand with your hands on
   your hips. Flex your neck
   toward your right shoulder.
   Hold for 10 seconds. Then
   flex your head toward your
   left shoulder and hold for 10
   seconds. Repeat five times.

Lower-Leg and Heel Stretch

Muscles stretched:
Gastrocnemius
Technique:
(The Achilles tendon is a large tendon con-
   necting the calf muscle to the heel.) Face a
   wall and stand approximately 3 feet in front
   of it with your feet several inches apart.
   Place your outstretched hands on the wall
   while keeping your feet flat on the floor.
   Gradually lean forward toward the wall,
   keeping your feet where they are. Hold the
   stretch for 10 seconds. Repeat five times.

Back Stretch

Muscles stretched:
Lower back, Gluteus, Hamstrings
Technique:
While lying on your back, grasp both
   of your legs behind the knees and
   gently pull the knees toward your chest.
   Hold for 10 seconds. Repeat 10 times.

Groin Stretch

Muscles stretched:
Adductors
Technique:
Sit on the floor with the soles of your feet touching in front of you. Leaning slightly forward, with your hands on your lower leg and your elbows resting on your inner thighs, slowly push your inner thighs closer to the floor. Hold the final stretched position for 10 seconds. Repeat five times. Each day try to push your inner thighs closer to the floor.

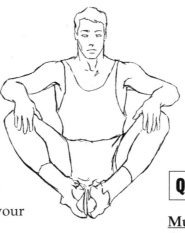

Quadriceps Stretch

Muscles stretched:
Quadriceps
Technique:
While lying on your right side, flex the knee of your left leg and grab the ankle with your left hand. Gradually move your hip forward until a good stretch is felt on the thigh. Hold for 10 seconds. Repeat five times. Repeat for the right leg while lying on your left side. *Caution:* Do not pull the ankle. Let the hip movement create the stretch.

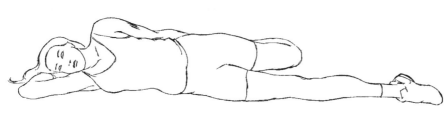

Lower-Back and Hip Stretch

Muscles stretched:
Lower back, Latissimus Dorsi
Technique:
Get down on all fours by placing your hands and knees on the floor. Lean back onto your heels. Extend your arms and place your chest on your thighs, allowing your shoulders to relax.

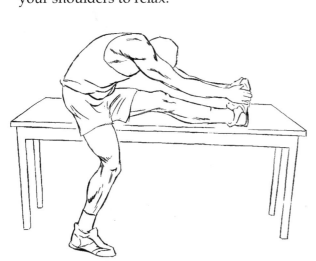

Hamstring Stretch

Muscles stretched:
Lower back, Hamstrings
Technique:
(The hamstring is a group of muscles in the upper leg that are important in knee flexion.) Sit on a table with one leg extended across the table and the opposite leg hanging over the side of the table. Bend forward at the waist and reach toward the toes of your extended leg. Bend the knee slightly. Reach gradually; do not bounce. Hold for 10 seconds. Repeat five times for each leg.

Lower-Back Stretch

Muscles stretched:
Lower back, Hamstrings
Technique:
While sitting on the floor with your legs
    extended out in front of you and your hands
    by your sides, slowly lower your chest
    toward your knees as far as you can go.
    Hold for 10 seconds. Repeat five times.

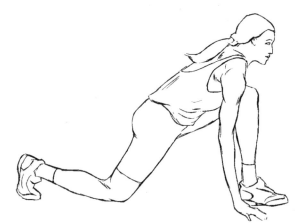

Leg and Groin Stretch

Muscles stretched:
Hip flexors, Rectus Femoris, Iliopsoas
Technique:
Move one leg forward until the knee of the
    front leg is directly over the ankle. Rest the
    back knee on the floor. Without changing
    leg position, lower the front hip downward
    to create a stretch. Hold for 10 seconds.
    Repeat five times. Change position and
    repeat for the other leg.

Back Extensor

Muscles stretched:
Lower back, Hamstrings
Technique:
Sit with your ankles crossed and your arms
    folded in front of you. Touch your chin to
    your chest. Roll forward and attempt to
    touch your forehead to your knees. Roll
    forward gradually, keeping your hips on
    the floor. Do not bounce. Hold for 10 sec-
    onds. Repeat five times.

Lower-Back Extensor

Muscles stretched:
Lower back
Technique:
Sit on a chair or bench with your feet flat on
    the floor and about six inches apart. Drop
    your chin and curl forward between your
    knees with your arms hanging toward the
    floor until you feel resistance in your back.
    Hold for 10 seconds. Repeat five times.

Hip Flexor Stretch

Muscles stretched:
Hamstrings, Gluteus
Technique:
Lie on your
    back on a table
    with your legs
    over the edge of the table. Bring your right
    knee to your chest. Use both of your hands
    under the knee joint to gradually bring the
    knee toward your armpit. Hold for 10
    seconds. Repeat five times for each leg.
    Caution: Do not apply downward pressure
    with your hand on the kneecap itself.

Shoulder and Arm Stretch

Muscles stretched:
Shoulder girdle
Technique:
Place both hands palms down and shoulder-
    width apart on a ledge or stationary bar.
    Bend knees slightly and let upper body
    drop down. Adjust height of hands and
    degree of knee bend to increase or decrease
    stretch. Hold for 10 seconds. Repeat five
    times.

Front-Leg Stretch

Muscles stretched:
Quadriceps
Technique:
Lean against a wall.
    Bring your left foot
    up behind you. Grasp
    the foot with your left hand
    and reach the foot toward
    your buttocks by pressing
    your left hip forward. Hold
    for 10 seconds. Repeat five
    times for each leg. *Caution:*
    do not pull on your ankle.
    Let the hip movement
    create the stretch.

Modified Hurdler Stretch

Muscles stretched:
Hamstrings, Gastrocnemius, Lower back
Technique:
Sit with your left leg extended
    and your right leg crossed
    in front with the heel near
    your crotch. Reach
    forward with both
    arms as far as
    possible. Bend left
    knee slightly. Hold
    for 10 seconds.
    Repeat five times
    for each leg.

Wall Lean and Heel Stretch

Muscles stretched:
Hamstrings,
  Gastrocnemius
Technique:
Stand about 3 feet from the wall,
  with one foot in front of the
  other. Bend the front knee
  slightly, and keep the back leg
  fully extended. Keep heels
  on the ground. Hold for 10
  seconds. Repeat for
  other leg.

Leaning Hamstring Stretch

Muscles stretched:
Lower back, Hamstrings
Technique:
While standing, raise one leg
  with the toes pointing up, and
  rest the heel of your foot on a
  solid object, for example, a
  car bumper or a bench. Begin
  with the leg in a bent position.
  Lean forward and reach with
  both arms toward raised foot.
  Hold for 10 seconds. Repeat
  five times for each leg.

Standing Arm and Leg Stretch

Muscles stretched:
Trunk, Shoulder
  girdle
Technique:
Stand with your feet
  shoulder-width apart.
  Raise your extended
  arms overhead. Place your
  weight on your toes and
  stretch to the sky. Hold for
  10 seconds. Repeat five times.

Forward-and-Back Arm Stretch

Muscles stretched:
Obliques, Back
Technique:
Stand with your
   feet shoulder-width apart. Bend
   forward about 20 degrees from the
   waist. Extend your left arm to the
   front and your right arm to the rear.
   Hold your arms shoulder high for
   10 seconds. Repeat five times. Then
   reverse arm positions and repeat five
   times.

Lying Arm and Leg Stretch

Muscles stretched:
Lower back
Technique:
Lie face down with your left arm extended
   above your head. Slowly raise your left arm
   and right leg simultaneously. Be careful not
   to arch your back. Hold for 6 seconds.
   Repeat five times for each side of body. (Not
   recommended for people with weak backs.)

High-Low Arm Stretch

Muscles stretched:
Shoulder girdle, Chest,
   Obliques
Technique:
Stand with your feet
   shoulder-width apart.
   Extend your left arm
   straight up from your
   body and extend your
   right arm straight down.
   Hold the stretch for 10
   seconds. Repeat five times.
   Then reverse arm positions
   and repeat five times.

Shoulder Stretch

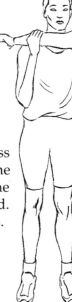

Muscles stretched:
Shoulder girdle, Triceps
Technique:
Bring arm, shoulder high, across
   the front of the body. Bend the
   elbow 90 degrees and grab the
   elbow with the opposite hand.
   Apply tension for 10 seconds.
   Repeat five times with
   each arm.

chapter 5

Developing a Cross-Training Program

Chapters 1 through 4 provided basic fitness principles to help you maximize your performance and select the training requirements unique to your specific sport. We recommend that you review each of these chapters and concentrate on those aspects of cross-training that are most important for you.

Many athletes have misconceptions about which exercises are important for their sport and how to work these into their training programs. Choosing proper exercises and using them at the proper time requires knowledge of the fitness demands of various sports, along with the knowledge of which exercises are most appropriate throughout the training cycle.

In chapters 6 through 31 we present cross-training options and recommendations that are geared toward 26 sports; activities that are similar to the sport in muscle and mechanical demands, yet are independent enough to provide the benefits of cross-training. Stretching exercises appropriate to the range and extent of movement for each sport are presented as well. In this chapter, we look at how to put the exercises and recommendations given in the remainder of the book to good use.

REVIEWING YOUR TRAINING GOALS

To get the most out of cross-training, you should first review the goals and objectives of your training program. Assess your strengths and weaknesses in your sport or activity and the specific demands of your sport, then look at which cross-training activities you can add to your program to enhance your overall potential. Your cross-training program will depend on the training goal you wish to establish and your present fitness and athletic ability.

Training goals vary considerably from sport to sport. The main goals of strength and power athletes should be to improve performance through increases in strength, and secondarily, to prevent injury. Endurance athletes also are concerned with improved performance, but injury prevention may concern them more when it comes to strength exercises. Athletes who seek increases in strength during their competitive period require weekly efforts of training with maximum resistance coupled with days of moderate- to light-load training.

Most sport training is divided into three seasons: off-season, pre-season, and in-season. The overall goal for most athletes is to peak in performance during competition. During the off-season, more time should be spent on high-volume training and less time on skill acquisition. As the pre-season approaches, volume should be reduced and higher training loads should be taken on to bring you to peak levels of strength and endurance. The highest loads are generally employed directly before competition with an adequate number of days (2-10) of unloading, gradually making workouts less intense to ensure recuperation prior to the competitive contest.

Sports with long seasons (e.g., basketball, baseball, volleyball) should have in-season programs to maintain peak and near-peak conditions for many months. Maintaining peak conditions can be a very difficult task. For those who rely on strength, weight training at heavy loads and low volume allows you to maintain a large percentage of your required strength during the competitive season. Athletes who are not yet at desired levels of strength during the competitive season may need to train two or more sessions a week utilizing high loads and low volume. Those who compete once a week should schedule their heavy load training two days after competition and moderately load two days before competition.

Custom design your training program for each season to help you reach and maintain peak performance for your sport.

Your current physical condition is very important when determining type and intensity of training loads. For example, if you are just starting a training program or have been in a detraining period, begin at a low intensity of strength and aerobic work and gradually build up. Fight the urge to do too much too soon. Knowing the strengths and weaknesses of your joints and muscle groups is also important. Muscle strength and endurance testing can identify muscle imbalance and allow the athlete to focus on weak areas.

INTEGRATING CROSS-TRAINING INTO YOUR TRAINING PROGRAM

The recommended exercises found in the cross-training matrix, strength, aerobic/anaerobic, and flexibility programs in each sport chapter are based on criteria specific to that sport and provide you with a variety of options depending on your needs. Some athletes may choose to work M-W-F on aerobic/anaerobic training and T-Th-Sat on strength training. Others may only need a one- or two-day strength training program combined with either a three-, five-, or seven-day aerobic/anaerobic program. Different sports require specific training programs:

The extent and intensity of any training program depends on the nature of the sport involved. For example, one might spend more time practicing golf or tennis skills than sprint swimming or running on account of the latter two being much more stressful to the body. Depending on your goals and where you are in your training cycle, you may want to cross-train on the same day you train for your primary sport. For example, you might work on flexibility and agility cross-training along with your primary-sport training in the morning and cross-train with plyometrics in the afternoon. At other times, you may want to cross-train on off days from your primary sport.

You may also substitute, depending on your specific needs, the type of cross-training exercise from those recommended in the matrix. So, if you are a soccer player who is having some leg or joint problems, you might substitute aqua jogging or cycling for StairMaster or Versa Climber. Feel free to experiment with different cross-training exercises in the matrix and the daily strength and aerobic/anaerobic programs until you find a comfortable fit for your sport and your body.

It is also important to be aware of—and to train for—the aerobic and anaerobic energy requirements for your sport. For this purpose, each sport chapter includes an aerobic/anaerobic training emphasis table that is based on an *approximation* of that sport's energy requirements. For example, the table for tennis on page 212 indicates your primary-sport training program should consist of exercise that is 10 percent aerobic, 20 percent combination aerobic and anaerobic, and 70 percent anaerobic. This emphasis can be achieved through your primary-sport training, or through a combination of your primary-sport and cross-training activities. During pre-season and in-season, your primary-sport training program may require 80 to 90 percent of your total training time, with the remaining 10 to 20 percent being spent on aerobic and anaerobic cross-training activities. During the off-season, however, you may want to focus more on cross-training, perhaps to avoid boredom or the chance of overuse injury. Of course, your training emphasis will change as your goals and needs change. For instance, a speed skater may wish to focus on increasing leg strength in the off-season by shading his program toward strength training. Now 40 to 50 percent of his training total may consist of cross-training activities for increasing muscular strength and power.

A general principle to follow in determining your overall training mix is first to evaluate the type of demands your sport places on your body. These demands determine the type of adaptation that has to take place. For example, athletes involved in high-speed events—sprint running, sprint swimming, ice hockey, and so on—should focus their program on strength and power training that requires muscular demands similar to that of the actual event. As you near your competitive season, your training should become more specific to your primary sport with cross-training making up approximately 25 to 30 percent of your weekly program. For the greatest gains in strength, power, and endurance, the level of your resistance, whether in your primary-sport activities or in your cross-training, should be as close to maximal as possible as the competition season nears.

During the off-season and in the early part of your training season, cross-training activities may make up as much as 50 percent of your training total. An exception is rehabilitation cross-training, which may require a greater percentage of the total. For example, a basketball player with a hairline fracture may

Exercise Transition

When making a transition from one type of exercise to another, different physiological and biomechanical demands are placed on the body. This may result in muscle soreness, stiffness, early onset of fatigue, and coordination problems. These symptoms should go away in a short time, however, if you use as a guide the following suggestions when crossing over to new exercises:

- Allow the body time to adjust to the new activity.
- Initially reduce volume and intensity of the activity.

- Allow at least three to four exercise sessions before progressing to a competitive level activity.
- Stretch the muscles specific to the sport before and after an activity.
- Allow one day's recovery between weight-training sessions involving similar muscle groups.

Try modifying the intensity and duration of the cross-training exercises when using them on the same day as your primary-sport training by using them to warm-up before practice, cool-down after practice, or for conditioning during exercise.

depend heavily on aqua jogging or cycling to maintain aerobic endurance and reduce the stress on the injury.

Now let's look at how an example athlete, in this case a long-distance runner, might put the cross-training for distance running chapter starting on page 88 to work.

Sample Cross-Training Program: Long-Distance Running

Say you are a 30-miles-per-week runner whose goal is to run a marathon in a target time of under three hours. Your primary goal might be to increase your aerobic endurance. Other goals might be to increase muscular strength and endurance and improve flexibility and agility. Although most sub-three-hour marathoners train an average of 70 miles per week or more for 12 weeks prior to the race, you may not be able to work up to such mileage due to weather conditions, tendency for injury with high mileage, or training schedule limitations. Instead, you could benefit from adding cross-training activities to your program.

Turning to the chapter on distance running (chapter 6), you'll find that the cross-training matrix highlights various ways cross-training can be used to improve each of the elements of fitness: strength, muscular endurance, aerobic and anaerobic endurance, and flexibility, with cross-training exercises and activities listed down the left side and cross-training elements listed across the top. Other areas are presented in the matrix as well including warm-up and cool-down, rehabilitation, and agility and balance.

The matrix shows that you may improve your aerobic capacity by using a number of cross-training activities, the most effective for runners being cross-country skiing, bicycling, and aqua jogging. Depending on how many miles you decide to train per week, you might want to alternate aerobic cross-training days with your primary-sport training days, or combine cross-training and running

Choose recommended activities from the cross-training matrix that fit your interests and needs.

on your lighter days. The sample aerobic/anaerobic programs on page 90 give you a number of options for incorporating activities on alternating days of a three-, five-, and seven-days-a-week program. Note that examples are given stressing lower body (LB), upper body (UB), and combined lower and upper body workouts (UB/LB). Feel free to follow one of these or trade them out for activities from the matrix you prefer. Again, to increase your aerobic fitness, it's important to cross-train within your target heart range for the duration of your exercise session.

Although marathon running depends primarily on the delivery of oxygen to the muscles via the aerobic energy system, competitors must also have the ability to sustain an anaerobic sprint at the end of the race. As you can see on the aerobic/anaerobic emphasis estimate table on page 90, anaerobic exercise should comprise approximately 5 percent of the total training time for marathoners. As mentioned in chapter 2, an effective means for promoting anaerobic endurance is interval training, where you alternate work periods of 30 seconds, 1 minute, and 2 minutes with recovery periods ranging from 1 to 15 minutes. A marathoner's approach to anaerobic interval training might look like this:

Work interval	Intensity level	Rest interval	Intervals per session
30 seconds	100%	1-2 minutes	8-18
1 minute	95-100%	3-5 minutes	5-15
2 minutes	90-100%	5-15 minutes	4-10

You may wish to interval train with running or try some cross-training activities such as working out on the treadmill, cross-country ski machine, and

Versa Climber. See page 86 for more information on other cross-training methods—such as the Fartlek technique—that can be used to train for both aerobic and anaerobic endurance.

Strength training is important for the marathon runner to maintain proper stride and prevent muscle fatigue. A strength program of three days per week where the focus is on the hips, legs, and upper body will help prevent injury and increase strength and endurance. Shoulder and arm strength are especially important in preventing fatigue late in the race. The strength training for runners program on page 91 focuses on the runner's specific needs. The matrix also suggests cross-training activities such as plyometrics and using resistance cords to help maintain strength in muscle groups essential to distance running.

The selection of the flexibility exercises for each sport is especially important. By increasing the range and extent of movement through stretching, you are better able to move from one exercise to another without increasing your chances of soreness or injury. Besides the specific exercises given on page 91, the cross-training matrix indicates that swimming and aerobic dance are good ways for long-distance runners to maintain and increase flexibility.

Table 5.1   Off-Season Training Program for a Distance Runner

Activity	Mon.	Tues.	Wed.	Thurs.	Fri.	Sat.	Sun.
Warm-up: Walk, slow jog, stretch	5-10 min.	5-10 min.	5-10 min.	5-10 min.	5-10 min.	5-10 min.	5-10 min.
Running (miles) total = 16-39	0-3 mi.	4-8 mi.	0-3 mi.	4-8 mi.	0-3 mi.	2-4 mi.	6-10 mi.
Aerobic/anaerobic cross-training	Swim 15-20 min.	Ex. bike (opt.)	Aqua jog 15-30 min.	Ex. bike (opt.)	Versa Climber or rowing machine 20-40 min.	Swim or aqua jog 15-20 min.	Ex. bike (opt.)
Weight training	5-7 exercises 15-40 min.		5-7 exercises 15-40 min.		5-7 exercises 15-40 min.		
Flexibility and plyometric exercises	Flex. 10-15 min.	F/Ply. 10-30 min.	Flex. 10-15 min.	F/Ply. 10-30 min.	Flex. 10-15 min.	F/Ply. 10-30 min.	Flex. 10-15 min.
Cool-down: Walk, stretch	5-10 min.	5-10 min.	5-10 min.	5-10 min.	5-10 min.	5-10 min.	5-10 min.
Cross-training time in addition to running	50-95 min.	20-50 min.	50-95 min.	20-50 min.	55-115 min.	35-70 min.	20-45 min.

Note: Tues/Thurs/Sun the exercise bike is suggested for warm-up/cool-down purposes and/or for additional aerobic training.

Table 5.1 shows how you as a competitive runner might put together an off-season training program that combines all these cross-training elements. Again, your training program will vary with your level of competitiveness, your specific goals, and where you are in your training cycle.

Now, say in the following year you decide to tackle some ultra-distance events such as the Western States 100-mile cross-country run. To achieve this goal, you should consider adding more strength training to your program to help prevent injuries. Focusing more on weight training along with plyometrics should help. If, in the next year, you decide to run shorter races (e.g., 10K [6.2 mile] runs), you should include more anaerobic work for speed development in your program. You will notice that the matrix recommends the treadmill, cross-country ski machine, Versa Climber, and lateral movement sports such as racquetball to enhance the anaerobic energy system.

Sample Cross-Training Program: Basketball

In a similar fashion, we have developed a sample off-season cross-training program for a basketball player (Table 5.2).

Table 5.2 Off-Season Training Program for a Basketball Player

Activity	Mon.	Tues.	Wed.	Thurs.	Fri.	Sat.	Sun.
Warm-up: Walk, exercise bike, stretch	5-10 min.	5-10 min.	5-10 min.	5-10 min.	5-10 min.	5-10 min.	5-10 min.
Aerobic/ anaerobic cross-training	Run 0-3 mi. 0-25 min.	Ex. bike 15-30 min.	Run 0-3 mi. 0-25 min.	Stair-Master 15-30 min.	Run 0-3 mi. 0-25 min.	Versa Climber 10-20 min.	Swim, Tennis, or Handball 15-30 min.
Weight training	6-8 exercises 15-35 min.		6-8 exercises 15-35 min.		6-8 exercises 15-35 min.		
Flexibility, agility, and plyometrics	Flex./ Agility 10-15 min.	Flex./ Plyom. 10-20 min.	Flex./ Agility 10-15 min.	Flex./ Plyom. 10-20 min.	Flex./ Agility 10-15 min.	Flex./ Plyom. 10-20 min.	
Basketball	Skills Practice 10-20 min.	Play 15-30 min.	Skills Practice 10-20 min.	Play 15-30 min.	Skills Practice 10-20 min.	Play 15-30 min.	Play 30-60 min.
Cool-down: Walk, ex. bike, stretch	5-10 min.	5-10 min.	5-10 min.	5-10 min.	5-10 min.	5-10 min.	5-10 min.
Total cross-training. time in addition to basketball	35-95 min.	35-70 min.	35-95 min.	35-70 min.	35-95 min.	30-60 min.	25-50 min.

Looking at the cross-training matrix in chapter 27 (basketball), you will find various activities highlighted as ways to improve each of the elements of fitness, as well as agility, and warm-up and cool-down.

The program outlined in Table 5.2 is very comprehensive as basketball relies on all elements of fitness as well as on skill development. This table is presented simply as an example and may not be appropriate for your needs. It is hoped, however, that you now understand the various ways to put together your program and can construct one that meets your needs and time availability.

OVERTRAINING AND BURNOUT

Many individuals have persisted in the unsubstantiated belief that improvements in strength, endurance, and skill are always proportional to the volume and intensity of the training program. In other words, the harder you work, the more you improve. It is possible, however, to get too much of a good thing.

Overtraining presents a paradox because many of the benefits associated with exercise are actually reversed in the individual who trains too much. While the athlete who trains two hours a day, five times a week may realize both a psychological and physical benefit, the athlete who trains four hours, seven days a week may suffer detrimental physical and psychological effects due to lack of adequate rest. Some signs of inadequate rest and recovery are loss of appetite, muscle tenderness, sleep problems, nausea, colds and allergic tendencies, and elevated blood pressure and heart rate.

Training stress, a common byproduct of the many demands made on athletes by rigorous training, may in some cases be beneficial; in others, detrimental. Negative adaptation to training stress may lead to conditions known as staleness and burnout and eventual withdrawal from participation. Staleness, brought on by overtraining, is the initial failure of the body to adjust to training stress. Staleness comprises both physiological and psychological symptoms including chronic fatigue, minor body aches, eating disorders, headaches, stomach upset, boredom, and anxiety. These are some factors that can contribute to staleness:

- Long training season
- Lack of social support
- Monotonous training program
- Rigorous training regimen
- Loss of self-confidence
- High competitive stress
- Perceived overload
- Boredom
- Perceived low accomplishment
- Unrealistic goal setting
- Low self-esteem

If the individual continues to train past staleness and cannot make the physical and mental adjustments to the demands, then there is the possibility of burnout. Burnout is an exhaustive physical, emotional, and mental response resulting from unsuccessful attempts to meet the demands of training stress. Burnout arises from a sense of distress and discontent and a perception of failing to achieve one's goals. After repeated efforts to attain these goals and after working as hard as possible without complete success, feelings of helplessness and hopelessness develop along with negative attitudes toward training and oneself.

Physically, the individual is in peak shape, but something just does not feel right. Enthusiasm has decreased; the athlete is bored and doesn't seem to make any progress. Those most prone to burnout are athletes who train too hard, too long, and too intensely and who are extremely dedicated to achieving the goals they have established. Unfortunately, overtraining and burnout sometimes lead the athlete to withdraw from training and competing altogether.

Prevention is the best way to guard against overtraining. The most efficient way to minimize the risk of too much stress on the body is to follow a cyclic training program that alternates easy, moderate, and hard periods of training. Designing a training program that provides the level of stress necessary for optimal improvement without exceeding one's physical and psychological tolerance is a difficult task. There are usually very few preliminary symptoms to warn

Mike Farmer

Among his accomplishments as basketball player and coach, Mike Farmer can boast an NCAA Basketball Championship in 1956 as a member of the San Francisco Dons; All-American Honors in 1958; third pick in the 1958 NBA draft by New York Knicks; eight years as an outstanding player in the NBA with the St. Louis Hawks, Cincinnati Royals, and Knicks; one year as head coach of the Philadelphia Warriors; and six years as an NBA scout.

Now retired from the NBA, Farmer volunteer-coaches both college and high school basketball and competes in biathlons. He's been cross-training for the past 17 years. His regime consists of weights, StairMaster, stationary bike, and water exercise. "To be the best you can be in one sport," says Farmer, "you need to train the whole body. Cross-training helps you reach this goal mentally as well as physically."

"As a coach, I can see a vast improvement in the ability of athletes over when I competed in the 1950s and 60s. When I retired in the late 60s, we were starting to do some weight training. With the teams I'm involved with now, it's a very big part of our training."

His advice is to start a program slowly and build a routine you can stay with for the long run—be consistent, don't start and stop. For athletes in competitive seasonal sports, cross-training can be used to augment regular training sessions. "Cross-training is a vital part of any competitive sports program to extend performance limits."

you that you are on the edge of becoming overtrained. Athletes who appear to be most susceptible to overtraining and staleness are those who attempt to always perform at their best during training *and* competition. Sudden increases in training volume and intensity may cause a physical and emotional overload in these types of athletes.

There is also some evidence that athletes who suddenly begin to perform at high levels during training may be on the verge of overtraining. They tend to feel so good during training that they overextend themselves, producing a performance breakdown. If you are overtrained, you may find a reduction in desire and enthusiasm for your sport. Day-to-day variations in muscle pain and sensations of fatigue, however, should not be confused with overtraining. These symptoms generally disappear in a short time.

Fortunately, staleness and burnout are not the end of the road. There are a variety of cross-training methods that can prevent, reduce, and, in many cases, eliminate the common problems that plague rigorous training programs. It is important for all of us who are engaged in rigorous physical training to have periodic breaks and to experiment with something different and fun to reduce the ever-present tension of practice.

Another important factor, especially for endurance athletes such as runners, cyclists, cross-country skiers, triathletes, and distance swimmers, is to consume a proper daily intake of carbohydrates to minimize the possibility of glycogen depletion that may lead to symptoms of overtraining. Ingestion of water or other hydrating fluids before and during competition is essential to prevent dehydration, especially in hot weather.

INJURY REHABILITATION

As mentioned in chapter 1, cross-training can be an important part of an athlete's rehabilitation program. For rehabilitating injured legs and feet, exercises such as cycling, rowing, and aqua jogging can be substituted for activities such as running, StairMaster, and rope jumping. A cross-country skier who is unable to ski because of an injury may aqua jog and cycle to maintain aerobic fitness until the injury has completely healed. These exercises also aid in maintaining muscular strength and endurance in the lower legs. Riding a bike for your warm-up an hour before running is a good way to ready your metabolism to switch over to fat burning during runs, while limiting stress on the lower body.

OFF-SEASON TRAINING: FOCUSING ON FUN

All athletes undergo physiological changes as the result of inactivity when their competitive season ends. You can, however, receive considerable benefits from a comprehensive off-season program that includes cross-training activities. Perhaps most important is for your off-season activities to be fun and enjoyable; cross-training can play an important role in helping to reduce boredom. Off-season cross-training programs also allow you to concentrate on weaknesses observed during competition. For example, swimmers might use off-season cross-training to increase upper body strength, soccer players to improve speed, and volleyball players to increase leg strength. *Remember:* Focus on having fun!

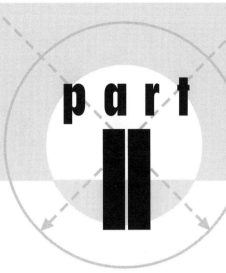

CROSS-TRAINING PROGRAMS

part

II

section
1

AEROBIC SPORTS PROGRAMS

Aerobic exercise is by necessity submaximal or prolonged exercise—energy must be delivered over a longer period of time. Aerobic power appears to be limited by cardiac output and the ability of the muscles to extract oxygen from the blood. Aerobic sports therefore depend primarily on the ability of the cardiorespiratory system to supply oxygen to the working muscles for energy production.

The major purpose in aerobic training is to produce certain biological adaptations in order to improve performance in your sport.

Your training must provide a sufficient overload of the cardiorespiratory system to stimulate an increase in heart function and endurance capacities of appropriate muscle groups. This requires adherence to a carefully planned and executed training program (see chapter 2 and chapter 5).

Aerobic activities reduce the likelihood of overuse injury by providing a period of rest and recovery for overworked muscles. They can also train and toughen accessory tissue (supporting ligaments and tendons) and reduce the risk of injury associated with muscle and balance. Aerobic activities such as aqua jogging or cycling can be valuable in rehabilitating and reducing stress on overused or injured tissue. Aerobic programs can also be used to increase or maintain the number of training workouts by reducing the stressful effects of an increase in training volume via the same training mode.

The aerobic training should involve rhythmic manipulation of the large muscles. Generally, maximum oxygen uptake by the muscles is reached at 95 percent of maximum heart rate or approximately 80 percent of maximum performance speed. The aerobic program should be progressively more difficult with increasing weeks and months of training. The body will adapt only to unaccustomed stress. It is important to remember that as the volume and intensity of training increases so does the risk of overuse injuries of soft tissue, joints, and bones.

Eventually, a plateau is reached during aerobic training when there is no longer a reduction in heart rate for a given load no matter how long you train. Although you may reach a limit of maximum oxygen uptake, you can still enhance your aerobic ability to work longer times at greater percentages of your maximum oxygen uptake. You must work at higher levels and elicit higher heart rates if you want to continue improving the capacity to persist in exercise at a higher percentage of your maximum oxygen uptake.

Although long-distance running, swimming, and cycling depend on the aerobic system to deliver oxygen to the muscles, competitors in these activities must also be able to sustain anaerobic sprints at the finish of events. Consequently, distance performers must not overlook the anaerobic aspects of training. Strength training is also essential for most aerobic sports, such as soccer, kayaking, or speed skating. Strong, well-balanced muscles are needed to support the skeletal structures in a proper biomechanical alignment that is so essential in running and cross-country skiing. Strong muscles also help to absorb shock and improve speed.

CROSS-TRAINING METHODS

There are three very effective methods for increasing aerobic endurance: continuous training, the Fartlek technique, and interval training.

Continuous training involves exercise at or near the same intensity as the actual competition. Continuous training is in fact overdistance training, allowing you to cover two to five times the distances of the actual event. Overload is achieved by increasing exercise duration. Because the recruitment of appropriate motor units is dependent on work rate, continuous training is ideally suited for endurance athletes.

Fartlek literally translated means *speed training* in Swedish. This program is suited for the out of doors over natural terrain. It consists of alternate endurance training at fast and slow speeds and does not require systematic manipulation of work and relief bouts unique to interval training. For example, middle- and long-distance cyclists, swimmers, and runners should practice short, fast distances at or below the eventual race pace. Track milers, for example, should run fast quarter miles and half miles in training in addition to downhill running and towing a parachute or resistance cord. Athletes generally determine their training scheme based on their own perceptual feelings of intensity and duration. The Fartlek technique is also an excellent off-season general conditioner and is good for anaerobic training as well.

Finally, interval training, is an extremely effective cross-training technique. Interval training uses high-intensity intermittent exercise for relatively long periods of time. Repeated exercise intervals with rest periods can vary from a few seconds to several minutes depending on your objectives. Intensity, duration, length of rest interval, the number of work intervals (repetitions), and the number of sets per workout can all be manipulated.

In this type of training, you proceed by alternating periods of relatively intense work (80-100 percent maximum heart rate levels) with active recovery (35-45 percent maximum heart rate). This allows for the performance of much more work at a more intense workload over a longer period of time than if working at your maximum heart rate continuously.

Training with interval techniques also allows you to be more sport specific during your training session. For example, a soccer player could run two sets of four 400-meter dashes under 70 seconds with a 2-minute, 20-second walking recovery between each dash. Heart rate would increase with this program up to 85 or 95 percent maximum heart rate (dashes) and fall to 35 and 45 percent during recovery (walking).

Distance Running

Distance runners use cross-training for a variety of reasons including training extension, warm-up and cool-down, strengthening for performance, and injury rehabilitation and prevention.

Distance running requires very high levels of aerobic endurance accompanied by strong leg muscles. Many runners use cycling and aqua jogging to increase aerobic endurance by reducing the stress on their leg muscles. A stationary bicycle can also be used for warm-up and cool-down exercises. Strength training for strong, balanced muscles to support the skeletal structure in a proper biomechanical alignment is essential to maintain proper stride and prevent unnecessary fatigue. Strong muscles will also help absorb the impact shock of training (approximately 1,700 steps per mile) and improve speed and stamina.

Many competitive runners run every day—some training two times a day on selected days. This type of training, in addition to long runs, can produce a significant buildup of exercise-released metabolites such as lactic acid in the muscles. A warm-up of low-resistance, high-cadence (60-75 or more revolutions per minute) cycling increases blood flow to the muscles and facilitates metabolite removal. A cool-down on the bike further flushes away the metabolites, reducing soreness and stiffness and enabling a quicker recovery and greater readiness for the next workout.

Aqua jogging has become an increasingly popular method—especially by university teams and top international athletes—of training through and rehabilitating lower extremities injuries in runners as a way of avoiding the stress of ground contact. Weight training and flexibility exercises are other rehabilitation tools for stretching and strengthening the injured area.

Cross-Training Activity Matrix

Key	Exercises	Strength	Muscular Endurance	Aerobic	Anaerobic	Warm-up/ Cool-down	Flexibility	Rehabilitation	Agility and Balance
T	Treadmill			◯	☆	◯		◯	
RM	Rowing Machine		◯	◯		◯			
XC	X-C Ski Machine		◯	◯	◯	◯		◯	
SM	StairMaster			◯		◯		◯	
VC	Versa Climber		☆	◯	◯	◯		◯	
B	Bicycling			☆	☆	☆		☆	
S	Swimming			◯		◯	◯		
AJ	Aqua Jogging			☆				☆	
A	Aerobics			◯			◯		
LS	Lateral Sports				◯				☆
WT	Weight Lifting	☆	☆				◯	☆	◯
P	Plyometrics	◯	◯						◯
AE	Arm Ergometer	◯	◯					◯	
RB	Roller Blading			◯	◯				◯
RJ	Rope Jumping			◯	◯				◯
AG	Agility Exercises								☆
F	Flexibility Exercises						☆	◯	

◯ = Recommended   ☆ = Highly Recommended

Aerobic/Anaerobic Sample Training Programs

3–Days–a–Week								
Program	1	2	3	4	5	6	7	Focus
1		R*		S		R		UB
2		R		AJ		RB		LB
3		R		XC		R		UB/LB

5–Days–a–Week								
Program	1	2	3	4	5	6	7	Focus
1	R	AE		R		RJ	R	UB
2	R	B		R		B	R	LB
3	R	VC		R		XC	R	UB/LB

7–Days–a–Week								
Program	1	2	3	4	5	6	7	Focus
1	R	S	R	RM	R	AJ	R	UB
2	R	B	R	RB	R	SM	R	LB
3	R	XC	R	SM	R	VC	R	UB/LB

*R = Running

Estimated Training Emphasis (percent)			
Aerobic	Anaerobic	Combination	Competition Distance
25	20	55	1 mi.
70	10	20	3 mi.
80	5	15	6 mi.
95		5	marathon

Weight Training Exercises

3-DAYS-A-WEEK

Inclined dumbbell fly
1 Set / 3-10 Reps
(see page 42)

Lateral pull down
1 Set / 3-10 Reps
(see page 44)

Alternate knee-touching sit-ups
1 Set / 25-75 Reps
(see page 48)

Tricep pulldowns
1 Set / 3-10 Reps
(see page 47)

Seated dumbbell curls
1 Set / 3–10 Reps
(see page 46)

Leg press
1 Set / 3–10 Reps
(see page 50)

Four-way hip exercises
1 Set / 10 Reps each exercise
(see pages 51-52)

Flexibility Exercises

Lower-leg and heel stretch
(see page 66)

Back stretch
(see page 66)

Groin stretch
(see page 67)

Quadriceps stretch
(see page 67)

Hamstring stretch
(see page 67)

Hip flexor stretch
(see page 69)

Distance Cycling

Distance cycling is primarily an aerobic, cardiorespiratory endurance sport. There are, however, periods such as hill climbs and sprints that add a significant anaerobic component to the event and these should be part of your training. Your cardiorespiratory endurance program should include intervals, hill training, and some sprint work as well as long endurance rides.

Cross-training can be of significant value to the cyclist in attaining greater strength, muscular endurance, and stamina. Strength is especially important in the quadriceps, hamstrings, gluteals, calves, lower back, and shoulder musculature. Increases in strength will improve performance, reduce the risk of high-use injuries, and decrease shoulder and back discomfort.

Cycling also demands superb balance and agility. Arm ergometry can be an excellent cross-training activity to increase arm strength and endurance. Long rides of over two or three hours demand high levels of muscular strength and endurance in order to maintain balance and control proper maneuvering.

Cross-Training Activity Matrix

Key	Exercises	Strength	Muscular Endurance	Aerobic	Anaerobic	Warm-up/Cool-down	Flexibility	Rehabilitation	Agility and Balance
T	Treadmill								
RM	Rowing Machine		○			○			
XC	X-C Ski Machine		○			○			
SM	StairMaster			○		○			
VC	Versa Climber		☆		☆	○			
S	Swimming			○		○	☆	○	
AJ	Aqua Jogging		○	☆				○	
A	Aerobics			○		○	○		
LS	Lateral Sports			○					☆
WT	Weight Training	☆	☆					☆	
P	Plyometrics	○	○						
AE	Arm Ergometer		☆		☆	○		○	
RB	Roller Blading		○	○	○				
RJ	Rope Jumping		○	○	○	○			
AG	Agility Exercises								☆
F	Flexibility Exercises						☆		
R	Running			○		○			

○ = Recommended   ☆ = Highly Recommended

Aerobic/Anaerobic Sample Training Programs

3–Days–a–Week							
Program	1	2	3	4	5	6	7	Focus
1		B*		SM		B		LB
2		B		VC		B		UB/LB
3		B		S		B		UB

5–Days–a–Week							
Program	1	2	3	4	5	6	7	Focus
1	B	RM		B		RJ	B	UB
2	B	VC		B		A	B	UB/LB
3	B	RB		B		SM	B	LB

7–Days–a–Week							
Program	1	2	3	4	5	6	7	Focus
1	B	SM	B	R	B	RB	B	LB
2	B	VC	B	AE	B	RM	B	UB
3	B	XC	B	RJ	B	A	B	UB/LB

*B = Cycling

Estimated Training Emphasis (percent)		
Aerobic	Anaerobic	Combination
80	5	15

Distance Cycling

Weight Training Exercises

3-DAYS-A-WEEK

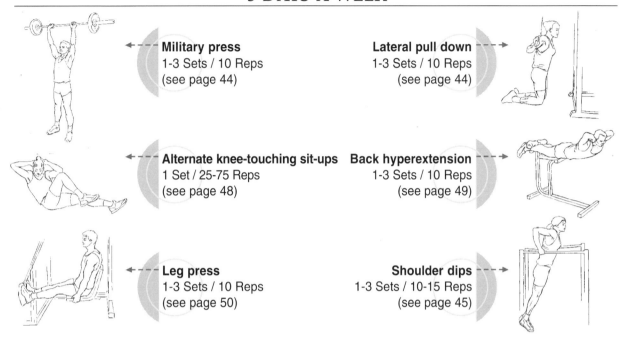

Military press
1-3 Sets / 10 Reps
(see page 44)

Lateral pull down
1-3 Sets / 10 Reps
(see page 44)

Alternate knee-touching sit-ups
1 Set / 25-75 Reps
(see page 48)

Back hyperextension
1-3 Sets / 10 Reps
(see page 49)

Leg press
1-3 Sets / 10 Reps
(see page 50)

Shoulder dips
1-3 Sets / 10-15 Reps
(see page 45)

ADDITIONAL EXERCISES (OPTIONAL)

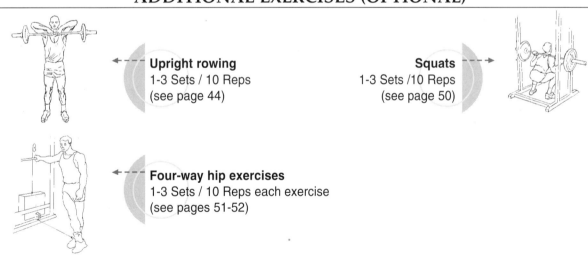

Upright rowing
1-3 Sets / 10 Reps
(see page 44)

Squats
1-3 Sets /10 Reps
(see page 50)

Four-way hip exercises
1-3 Sets / 10 Reps each exercise
(see pages 51-52)

Flexibility Exercises

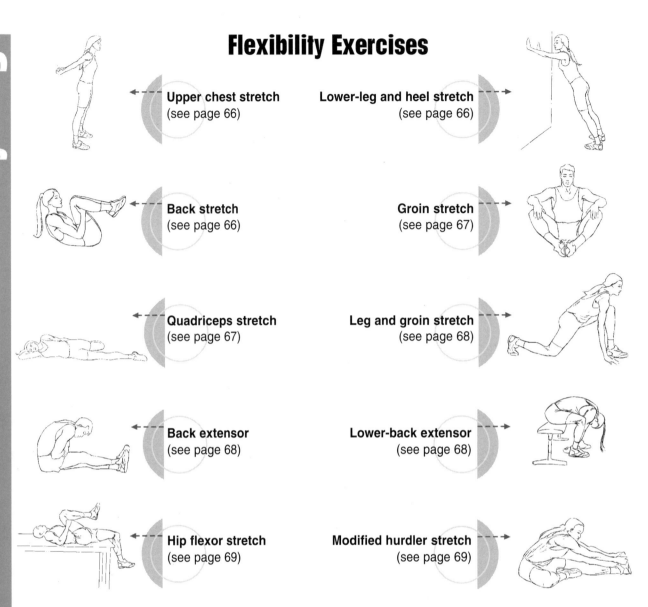

Upper chest stretch
(see page 66)

Lower-leg and heel stretch
(see page 66)

Back stretch
(see page 66)

Groin stretch
(see page 67)

Quadriceps stretch
(see page 67)

Leg and groin stretch
(see page 68)

Back extensor
(see page 68)

Lower-back extensor
(see page 68)

Hip flexor stretch
(see page 69)

Modified hurdler stretch
(see page 69)

Distance Swimming

Distance swimming places great demands on the aerobic energy system. In addition, strong arm, shoulder, and leg muscles are not only important for power propulsion but also for efficient body alignment in the water as well.

Strength training has been a part of competitive swimmers' training regimens for many years. Swimmers know that swimming alone will not produce the muscle strength and endurance necessary for high performance levels. Improving your strength can also increase the muscular endurance and power of your stroke and kick. Cardiorespiratory endurance can be supplemented with exercises using the Versa Climber, StairMaster, upper body ergometer, and cross-country ski machine as well as by aerobics. Flexibility in the shoulder and hips is very important in maintaining a smooth stroke and kick as well as in preventing muscle soreness and injuries.

Swimmers should perform kicking and pulling drills with resistance cords in order to isolate and overload their arms and legs so that each will make a contribution when the whole stroke is swum in competition.

The best form of primary-sport training for distance swimmers consists primarily of long swims and short rest, under-distance repeats because this improves aerobic capacity. Distance swimmers also need to improve the anaerobic capacity of muscles so they can swim faster in the final portions of the races. You must be able to sprint when fatigued. Training for late-race sprint swimming should consist of speeds specific to late-race conditions with sets of 50, 100, and 200 meters. Running sprints to improve anaerobic capacity may be used to alternate with in-water training.

Distance Swimming

Cross-Training Activity Matrix

Key	Exercises	Strength	Muscular Endurance	Aerobic	Anaerobic	Warm-up/ Cool-down	Flexibility	Rehabilitation	Agility and Balance
T	Treadmill					○			
RM	Rowing Machine		○						
XC	X-C Ski Machine		○	○		○			
SM	StairMaster			○					
VC	Versa Climber		☆	○	○	☆			
B	Bicycling			○				○	
AJ	Aqua Jogging			○					
A	Aerobics		○	○			○		○
LS	Lateral Sports		○						○
WT	Weight Training	☆	☆				○	☆	
P	Plyometrics	○	○	○					
AE	Arm Ergometer	☆	☆	○				○	
RB	Roller Blading			○					
RJ	Rope Jumping			○					
AG	Agility Exercises								
F	Flexibility Exercises						☆		
R	Running			○					

○ = Recommended   ☆ = Highly Recommended

98

Aerobic/Anaerobic Sample Training Programs

3–Days–a–Week							
Program	1	2	3	4	5	6	7	Focus
1		S*		VC		S		UB
2		S		SM		S		LB
3		S		RJ		S		UB/LB

5–Days–a–Week							
Program	1	2	3	4	5	6	7	Focus
1	S	SM		S		B	S	LB
2	S	XC		S		VC	S	UB/LB
3	S	AE		S		RM	S	UB

7–Days–a–Week							
Program	1	2	3	4	5	6	7	Focus
1	S	SM	S	RB	S	B	S	LB
2	S	VC	S	RJ	S	XC	S	UB/LB
3	S	RM	S	A	S	AE	S	UB

*S = Swimming

Estimated Training Emphasis (percent)			
Aerobic	Anaerobic	Combination	Competition Distance
5	30	65	200 meters
25	20	55	400 meters
70	10	20	1500 meters

Weight Training Exercises

3-DAYS-A-WEEK

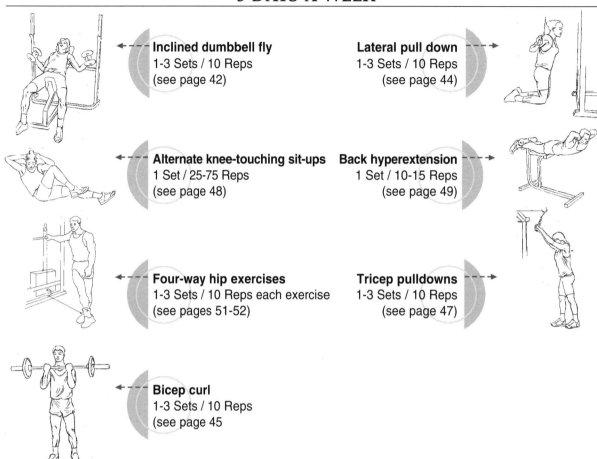

Inclined dumbbell fly
1-3 Sets / 10 Reps
(see page 42)

Lateral pull down
1-3 Sets / 10 Reps
(see page 44)

Alternate knee-touching sit-ups
1 Set / 25-75 Reps
(see page 48)

Back hyperextension
1 Set / 10-15 Reps
(see page 49)

Four-way hip exercises
1-3 Sets / 10 Reps each exercise
(see pages 51-52)

Tricep pulldowns
1-3 Sets / 10 Reps
(see page 47)

Bicep curl
1-3 Sets / 10 Reps
(see page 45

Flexibility Exercises

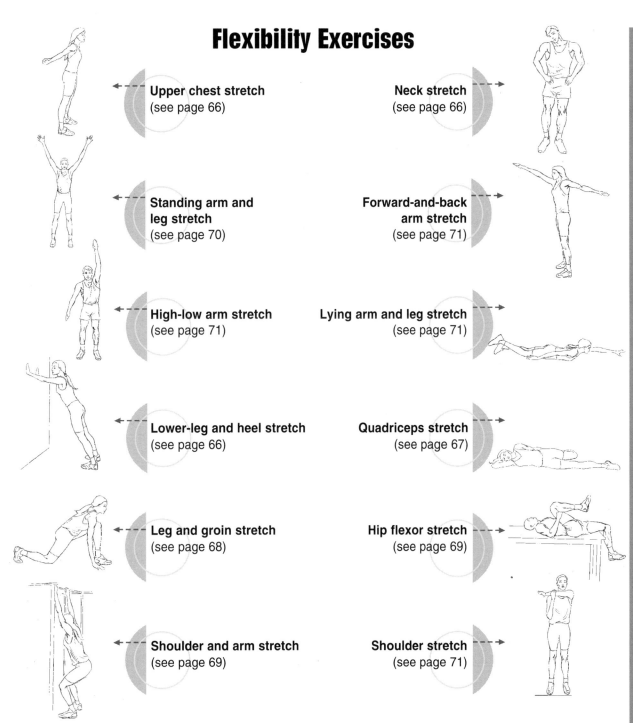

Upper chest stretch
(see page 66)

Neck stretch
(see page 66)

Standing arm and
leg stretch
(see page 70)

Forward-and-back
arm stretch
(see page 71)

High-low arm stretch
(see page 71)

Lying arm and leg stretch
(see page 71)

Lower-leg and heel stretch
(see page 66)

Quadriceps stretch
(see page 67)

Leg and groin stretch
(see page 68)

Hip flexor stretch
(see page 69)

Shoulder and arm stretch
(see page 69)

Shoulder stretch
(see page 71)

Triathlon/ Duathlon

The triathlon and duathlon, by the very nature of their 2-3 combined sports, are cross-training events. The triathlon is in some ways the epitome of cardiorespiratory cross-training. We have highlighted in the matrix some additional types of cardiorespiratory exercises for your consideration when you need a mental or physical break from the big 3—swimming, biking, and running—as well as to help avoid overuse injury.

The triathelete's greatest challenge is to fit it all in and still have a semblance of a normal life. The strength training is therefore presented as a split routine after six shorter workouts. These can be combined into a three-day program if you desire.

We also suggest that you superset your weight training to save additional time. To superset, you perform a set of one exercise followed by an exercise of another muscle group, then rest. This cuts down on the rest time needed between sets.

Cross-Training Activity Matrix

Key	Exercises	Strength	Muscular Endurance	Aerobic	Anaerobic	Warm-up/ Cool-Down	Flexibility	Rehabilitation	Agility and Balance
T	Treadmill			○	○	○			
RM	Rowing Machine		○	○	○	○			
XC	X-C Ski Machine			○	○	○			
SM	StairMaster			○		○			
VC	Versa Climber		☆		☆	○			
B	Bicycling			○	○	○			
S	Swimming			○	○		○		
AJ	Aqua Jogging			☆				☆	
A	Aerobics			○			○		○
LS	Lateral Sports				○				○
WT	Weight Training	☆	☆					☆	
P	Plyometrics	○	○					○	
AE	Arm Ergometer		○	○	○				
RB	Roller Blading			○					○
RJ	Rope Jumping			○		○			○
AG	Agility Exercises				○				○
F	Flexibility Exercises					○	○		
R	Running			○	○	○			

○ = Recommended   ☆ = Highly Recommended

TRIATHLON

Aerobic/Anaerobic Sample Training Programs

6–Days–a–Week (3 Days of Cross-Training)

Program	1	2	3	4	5	6	7	Focus
1	VC	R	XC	S	RJ	B		UB
2	RM	R/S	AJ	B/S	RB	R/B		LB
3	A	S/B	LS	S/R	AG	B/R		UB/LB

7–Days–a–Week (3 Days of Cross-Training)

Program	1	2	3	4	5	6	7	Focus
1	VC	R (long)	XC	S (long)	RJ	B (long)	R/B/S	UB
2	RB	R (long)	SM	S (long)	AJ	B (long)	S/B/R	LB
3	AG	R (long)	LS	S (long)	P	B (long)	B/R/S	UB/LB

7 Days-a-Week Heavy Load

Program	1	2	3	4	5	6	7	Focus
1	B/S AE	R (long)	S/R VC	S (long)	R/B XC	B (long)	B/R/S	UB
2	B/S	R (long) AJ	S/R	S (long) RB	R/B	B (long) SM	S/B/R	LB
3	B/S A	R (long)	S/R LS	S (long)	R/B AG or P	B (long)	R/B/S	UB/LB

Recommended only for experienced, highly trained triathletes.

DUATHLON
Aerobic/Anaerobic Sample Training Programs

Program	1	2	3	4	5	6	7	Focus
3–Days–a–Week								
1		R		B		R		LB
2		B		R		B		LB
3		R		B/R		B		LB

Program	1	2	3	4	5	6	7	Focus
5–Days–a–Week								
1	R	SM		B		RB	R/B	LB
2	R	VC		B		XC	R/B	UB/LB
3	R	AE		B		RM	R/B	UB

Program	1	2	3	4	5	6	7	Focus
7–Days–a–Week								
1	R/B (long)	RB	R (long)	AJ	R (easy)	B (long)	AJ	LB
2	R/B (long)	XC	R (long)	RM	R (easy)	B (long)	VC	UB
3	R/B (long)	A	R (long)	LS	R (easy)	B (long)	RB	UB/LB

Weight Training Exercises

3-DAYS-A-WEEK

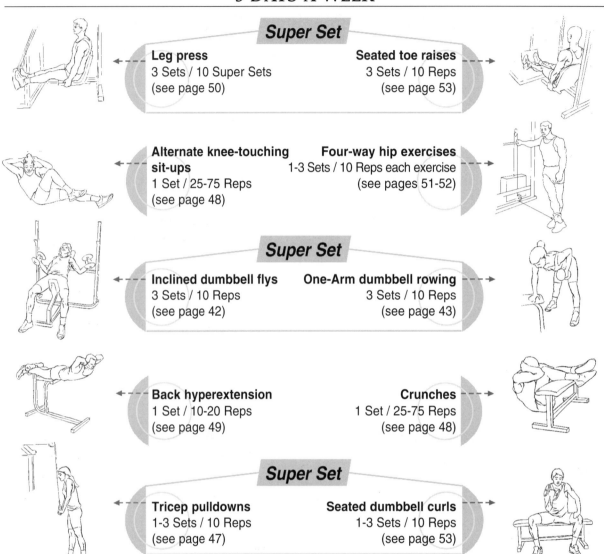

Super Set

Leg press
3 Sets / 10 Super Sets
(see page 50)

Seated toe raises
3 Sets / 10 Reps
(see page 53)

**Alternate knee-touching
sit-ups**
1 Set / 25-75 Reps
(see page 48)

Four-way hip exercises
1-3 Sets / 10 Reps each exercise
(see pages 51-52)

Super Set

Inclined dumbbell flys
3 Sets / 10 Reps
(see page 42)

One-Arm dumbbell rowing
3 Sets / 10 Reps
(see page 43)

Back hyperextension
1 Set / 10-20 Reps
(see page 49)

Crunches
1 Set / 25-75 Reps
(see page 48)

Super Set

Tricep pulldowns
1-3 Sets / 10 Reps
(see page 47)

Seated dumbbell curls
1-3 Sets / 10 Reps
(see page 53)

Flexibility Exercises

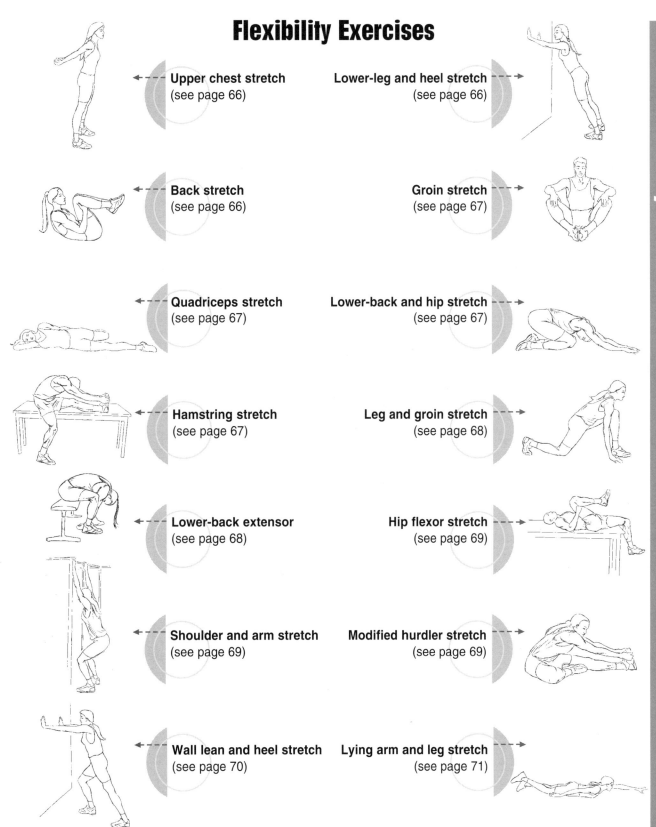

Upper chest stretch
(see page 66)

Lower-leg and heel stretch
(see page 66)

Back stretch
(see page 66)

Groin stretch
(see page 67)

Quadriceps stretch
(see page 67)

Lower-back and hip stretch
(see page 67)

Hamstring stretch
(see page 67)

Leg and groin stretch
(see page 68)

Lower-back extensor
(see page 68)

Hip flexor stretch
(see page 69)

Shoulder and arm stretch
(see page 69)

Modified hurdler stretch
(see page 69)

Wall lean and heel stretch
(see page 70)

Lying arm and leg stretch
(see page 71)

Cross-Country Skiing

There are two basic types of cross-country skiing: classical and free style, or skating, techniques. Classical skiing provides the skier with the basic techniques for moving straight forward in tracks. In the free style, or skating style, the skier places the skis in a distinctive V-shape and, similar to ice skating, pushes at an angle in the power phase rather than straight ahead in the tracks.

Both techniques require not only a high level of leg and arm strength, but both place the greatest physiological demands on the cardiorespiratory system of any sport. Cross-country skiers must possess the aerobic potential for prolonged exertion and, at the same time, must maintain anaerobic ability for breaking away from others and climbing steep terrain.

Cross-training exercises can be of great value in helping the cross-country skier develop muscle strength and endurance and increased aerobic capacity. Your strength training should duplicate as much as possible the movement pattern that you use while skiing. For muscular endurance training, try to duplicate the speed of movement and resistance of cross-country skiing in your exercises as closely as possible.

Cross-Training Activity Matrix

Key	Exercises	Strength	Muscular Endurance	Aerobic	Anaerobic	Warm-up/ Cool-down	Flexibility	Rehabilitation	Agility and Balance
T	Treadmill			◐					
RM	Rowing Machine		◐	◐	◐	◐		◐	
XC	X-C Ski Machine		◐	☆	☆				
SM	StairMaster		◐	◐	◐				
VC	Versa Climber	☆	◐	☆	◐				
B	Bicycling		◐	◐	◐	☆			
S	Swimming			◐			◐	◐	
AJ	Aqua Jogging			◐				◐	
A	Aerobics			◐					◐
LS	Lateral Sports								◐
WT	Weight Training	☆	☆					◐	
P	Plyometrics	◐	◐						
AE	Arm Ergometer	◐	◐						
RB	Roller Blading			☆	☆				
RJ	Rope Jumping			◐	◐				
AG	Agility Exercises								◐
F	Flexibility Exercises							◐	
R	Running			◐	◐				

◐ = Recommended ☆ = Highly Recommended

Cross-Country Skiing

Aerobic/Anaerobic Sample Training Programs

3–Days–a–Week								
Program	**1**	**2**	**3**	**4**	**5**	**6**	**7**	**Focus**
1		SK*		B		SK		LB
2		SK		RM		SK		UB
3		SK		VC		SK		UB/LB

5–Days–a–Week								
Program	**1**	**2**	**3**	**4**	**5**	**6**	**7**	**Focus**
1	SK	SM		SK		RB	SK	LB
2	SK	VC		SK		RJ	SK	UB/LB
3	SK	A		SK		LS	SK	UB/LB

7–Days–a–Week								
Program	**1**	**2**	**3**	**4**	**5**	**6**	**7**	**Focus**
1	SK	VC	SK	AJ	SK	RJ	SK	UB/LB
2	SK	P	SK	VC	SK	AE	SK	UB
3	SK	SM	SK	B	SK	R	SK	LB

*SK = Cross-country skiing

Estimated Training Emphasis (percent)		
Aerobic	**Anaerobic**	**Combination**
85	15	

Weight Training Exercises

3-DAYS-A-WEEK

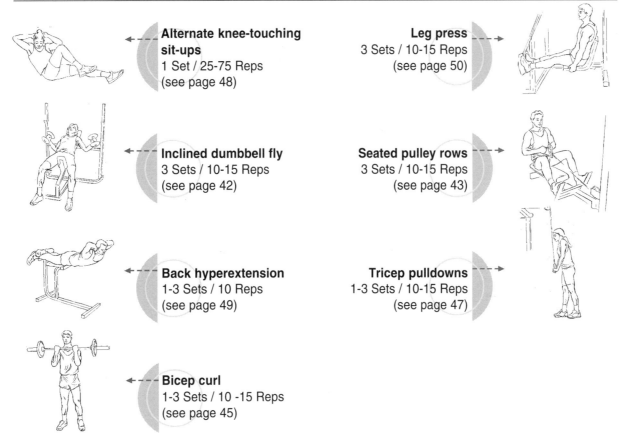

Alternate knee-touching sit-ups
1 Set / 25-75 Reps
(see page 48)

Leg press
3 Sets / 10-15 Reps
(see page 50)

Inclined dumbbell fly
3 Sets / 10-15 Reps
(see page 42)

Seated pulley rows
3 Sets / 10-15 Reps
(see page 43)

Back hyperextension
1-3 Sets / 10 Reps
(see page 49)

Tricep pulldowns
1-3 Sets / 10-15 Reps
(see page 47)

Bicep curl
1-3 Sets / 10 -15 Reps
(see page 45)

ADDITIONAL EXERCISES (OPTIONAL)

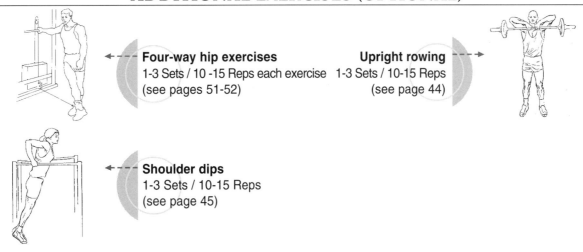

Four-way hip exercises
1-3 Sets / 10 -15 Reps each exercise
(see pages 51-52)

Upright rowing
1-3 Sets / 10-15 Reps
(see page 44)

Shoulder dips
1-3 Sets / 10-15 Reps
(see page 45)

Flexibility Exercises

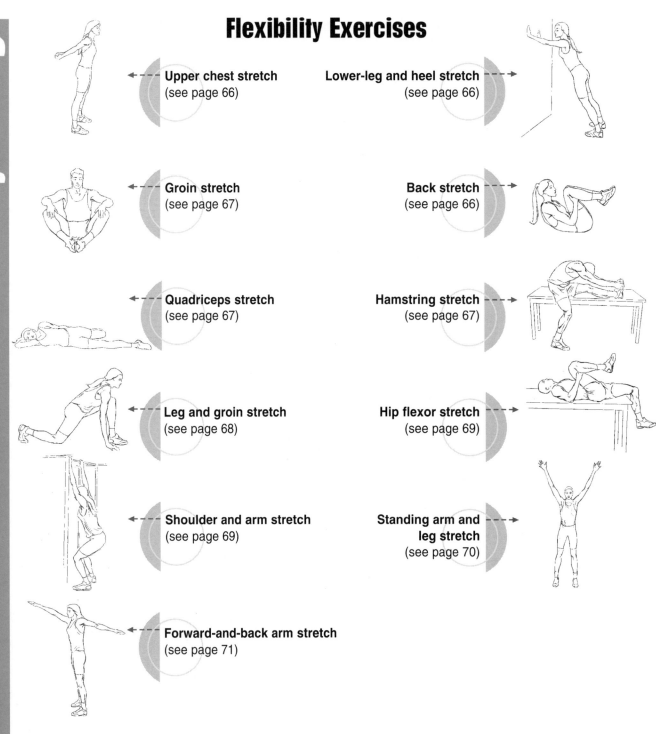

Upper chest stretch (see page 66)

Lower-leg and heel stretch (see page 66)

Groin stretch (see page 67)

Back stretch (see page 66)

Quadriceps stretch (see page 67)

Hamstring stretch (see page 67)

Leg and groin stretch (see page 68)

Hip flexor stretch (see page 69)

Shoulder and arm stretch (see page 69)

Standing arm and leg stretch (see page 70)

Forward-and-back arm stretch (see page 71)

Cross-Country Skiing

112

11

Soccer

Soccer is a vigorous game requiring players to have a great deal of speed, cardiorespiratory endurance, and leg strength. The main skills needed are running and kicking. Soccer players also must be able to start, stop, and change direction quickly. Soccer requires that players be able to perform at a high rate of speed over a prolonged period of time. There are a variety of cross-training options that meet these needs.

Cross-training exercises such as distance running, cycling, and aqua jogging are excellent for building aerobic endurance. Agility and balance are also keys to success in soccer. Activities such as lateral running, shuttle runs, zigzag running, and racquetball can be helpful in these two areas.

Some specific needs in soccer by position are as follows:

- Goalkeepers: Leg and thigh strength, upper body and shoulder strength, and jumping power
- Strikers and stoppers: Leg and thigh strength, jumping power strength, neck strength, heading ability, and cardiorespiratory endurance
- Fullbacks, midfielders, and wings: Leg and thigh strength, muscular endurance, and cardiorespiratory endurance

Cross-Training Activity Matrix

Key	Exercises	Strength	Muscular Endurance	Aerobic	Anaerobic	Warm-up/ Cool-down	Flexibility	Rehabilitation	Agility and Balance
T	Treadmill			○	○	○			
RM	Rowing Machine		○	○	○	○			
XC	X-C Ski Machine			○		○			
SM	StairMaster			○		○			
VC	Versa Climber		○		○	○			
B	Bicycling		○	☆	☆	☆			
S	Swimming			○			○	○	
AJ	Aqua Jogging			○				☆	
A	Aerobics			○		○	○		○
LS	Lateral Sports				○				○
WT	Weight Training	☆	☆					☆	
P	Plyometrics	○	○					○	
AE	Arm Ergometer			○	○				
RB	Roller Blading			○	○				○
RJ	Rope Jumping			○	○	○			○
AG	Agility Exercises				○				○
F	Flexibility Exercises					○	○		
R	Running			☆	☆				

○ = Recommended   ☆ = Highly Recommended

Aerobic/Anaerobic Sample Training Programs

3–Days–a–Week								
Program	**1**	**2**	**3**	**4**	**5**	**6**	**7**	**Focus**
1		R*		SM		R		LB
2		R		XC		R		UB/LB
3		R		AE		R		UB

5–Days–a–Week								
Program	**1**	**2**	**3**	**4**	**5**	**6**	**7**	**Focus**
1	R	SM		R		B	R	LB
2	R	VC		R		RM	R	UB
3	R	RJ		R		A	R	UB/LB

7–Days–a–Week								
Program	**1**	**2**	**3**	**4**	**5**	**6**	**7**	**Focus**
1	R	SM	R	B	R	RB	R	LB
2	R	A	R	XC	R	RJ	R	UB/LB
3	R	RM	R	VC	R	P	R	UB

*R = Running or soccer

Estimated Training Emphasis (percent)		
Aerobic	**Anaerobic**	**Combination**
20	60	20

Weight Training Exercises

3-DAYS-A-WEEK

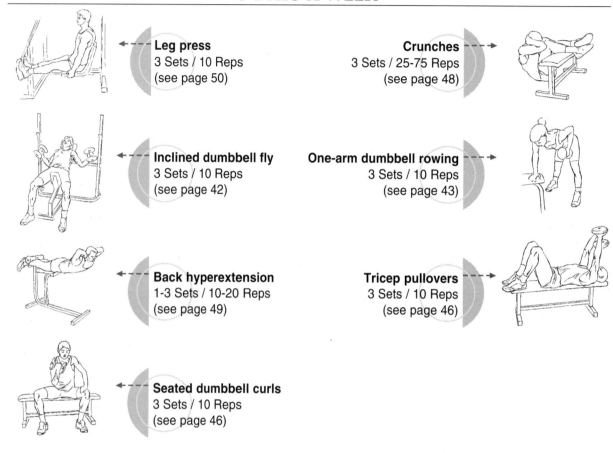

Leg press
3 Sets / 10 Reps
(see page 50)

Crunches
3 Sets / 25-75 Reps
(see page 48)

Inclined dumbbell fly
3 Sets / 10 Reps
(see page 42)

One-arm dumbbell rowing
3 Sets / 10 Reps
(see page 43)

Back hyperextension
1-3 Sets / 10-20 Reps
(see page 49)

Tricep pullovers
3 Sets / 10 Reps
(see page 46)

Seated dumbbell curls
3 Sets / 10 Reps
(see page 46)

ADDITIONAL EXERCISES (OPTIONAL)

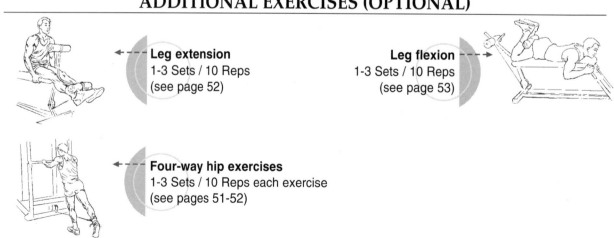

Leg extension
1-3 Sets / 10 Reps
(see page 52)

Leg flexion
1-3 Sets / 10 Reps
(see page 53)

Four-way hip exercises
1-3 Sets / 10 Reps each exercise
(see pages 51-52)

Flexibility Exercises

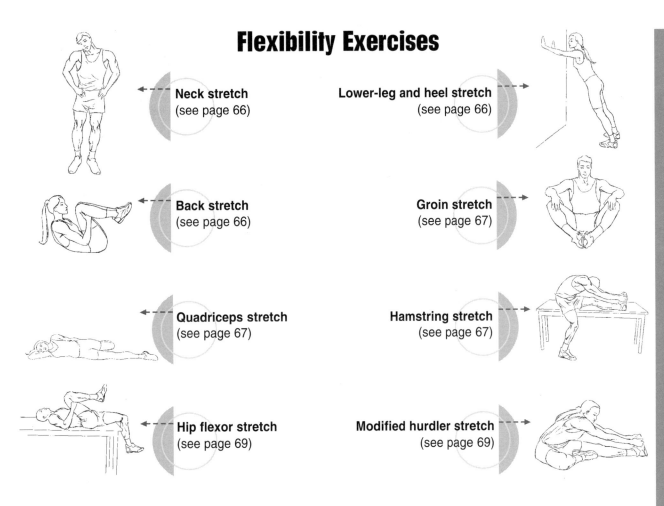

Neck stretch
(see page 66)

Lower-leg and heel stretch
(see page 66)

Back stretch
(see page 66)

Groin stretch
(see page 67)

Quadriceps stretch
(see page 67)

Hamstring stretch
(see page 67)

Hip flexor stretch
(see page 69)

Modified hurdler stretch
(see page 69)

12

Rowing, Kayaking, and Paddling

The primary fitness elements these activities rely on are cardiorespiratory endurance and muscular endurance. Strength training, however, can be very helpful in the noncompetitive season as a means of increasing your muscle mass. This, coordinated with other aspects of your training, can facilitate greater muscular endurance. Good flexibility can decrease the likelihood of injury and is important if you intend to continue in this sport for many years. A good warm-up that focuses on loosening up the arms, back, and shoulder girdle and a thorough cool-down will also enhance your training by gradually stimulating the heart before exercise and maintaining blood flow back to the heart during exercise.

Even though the goal in rowing, kayaking, and paddling is to propel the boat through the water, they all vary considerably in their fitness demands. Rowing is primarily aerobic with short periods of anaerobic energy required at the start and finish of the races. The demands on shoulders, arms, and hamstrings are very high. Kayaking and paddling competitively require greater amounts of anaerobic endurance than does rowing.

Cross-training methods such as arm ergometry, Versa Climber, and rowing machines are excellent for developing upper body strength. Aerobic activities for rowing include cross-country ski machines, StairMaster, and aerobics. For conditioning the anaerobic system for paddling and kayaking, plyometric activities such as medicine ball throwing, fast aqua jogging, and weight-resistant cords are useful.

Cross-Training Activity Matrix

Key	Exercises	Strength	Muscular Endurance	Aerobic	Anaerobic	Warm-up/ Cool-down	Flexibility	Rehabilitation	Agility and Balance
T	Treadmill			○		○			
RM	Rowing Machine		☆	☆	☆			○	
XC	X-C Ski Machine			○					
SM	StairMaster			○					
VC	Versa Climber		☆	☆	☆				
B	Bicycling			○	○	☆	○		
S	Swimming			○		○			
AJ	Aqua Jogging			○	○		○		
A	Aerobics			○					○
LS	Lateral Sports				○				○
WT	Weight Training	☆	☆					☆	
P	Plyometrics	○							
AE	Arm Ergometer		☆		○				
RB	Roller Blading			○					
RJ	Rope Jumping			○	○				
AG	Agility Exercises								○
F	Flexibility Exercises						○		
R	Running			○	○				

○ = Recommended   ☆ = Highly Recommended

Rowing, Kayaking, and Paddling

Aerobic/Anaerobic Sample Training Programs

3–Days–a–Week							
Program	1	2	3	4	5	6	7	Focus
1		RW*		AE		RW		UB
2		RW		SM		RW		LB
3		RW		VC		RW		UB/LB

5–Days–a–Week							
Program	1	2	3	4	5	6	7	Focus
1	RW	AE		RW		RM	RW	UB
2	RW	XC		RW		VC	RW	UB/LB
3	RW	B		RW		SM	RW	LB

7–Days–a–Week							
Program	1	2	3	4	5	6	7	Focus
1	RW	AE	RW	RM	RW	P	RW	UB
2	RW	SM	RW	B	RW	RB	RW	LB
3	RW	VC	RW	AJ	RW	RJ	RW	UB/LB

*RW = rowing

Estimated Training Emphasis (percent)		
Aerobic	Anaerobic	Combination
50	20	30

Weight Training Exercises

3-DAYS-A-WEEK

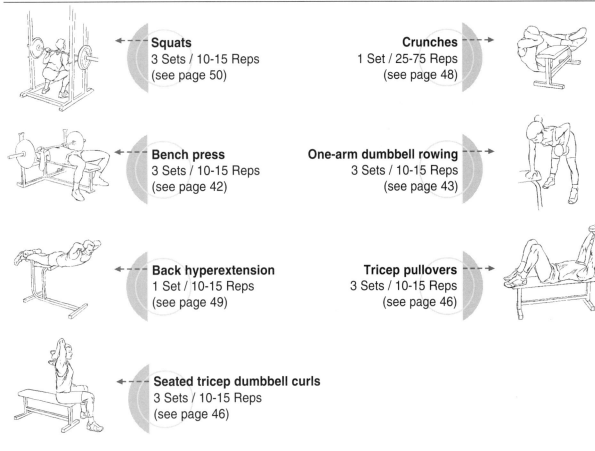

Squats
3 Sets / 10-15 Reps
(see page 50)

Crunches
1 Set / 25-75 Reps
(see page 48)

Bench press
3 Sets / 10-15 Reps
(see page 42)

One-arm dumbbell rowing
3 Sets / 10-15 Reps
(see page 43)

Back hyperextension
1 Set / 10-15 Reps
(see page 49)

Tricep pullovers
3 Sets / 10-15 Reps
(see page 46)

Seated tricep dumbbell curls
3 Sets / 10-15 Reps
(see page 46)

ADDITIONAL EXERCISES (OPTIONAL)

Military press
1-3 Sets / 10-15 Reps
(see page 44)

Four-way hip exercises
1-3 Sets / 10 Reps each exercise
(see pages 51-52)

Rowing, Kayaking, and Paddling

Flexibility Exercises

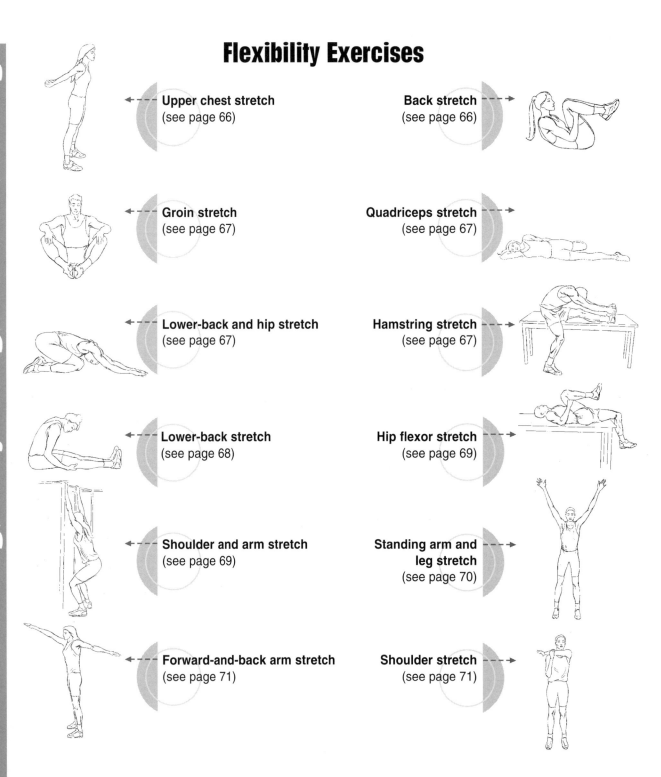

Upper chest stretch
(see page 66)

Back stretch
(see page 66)

Groin stretch
(see page 67)

Quadriceps stretch
(see page 67)

Lower-back and hip stretch
(see page 67)

Hamstring stretch
(see page 67)

Lower-back stretch
(see page 68)

Hip flexor stretch
(see page 69)

Shoulder and arm stretch
(see page 69)

Standing arm and leg stretch
(see page 70)

Forward-and-back arm stretch
(see page 71)

Shoulder stretch
(see page 71)

In-Line and Speed Skating

In-line skating, or roller blading, is an exhilarating new sport that is rapidly becoming more and more popular. The skill and muscles involved are very close to those used in speed skating. Strong leg muscles are needed for maintaining force and preventing fatigue. Fatigued muscles in the later phases of a contest may result in a loss of balance and coordination. Both sports require strength, speed, agility, and aerobic endurance. Also, anaerobic endurance is vital for quick sprints at the end of a race.

The cross-training program for in-line and speed skating should focus on quick, powerful bursts of activity, important in starting and finishing, along with lower-intensity types of aerobic exercise for longer distances.

Speed skating requires very precise balance, especially on the turns when the slightest mistake can lead to a fall. Unlike speed skating, where injuries from a fall are limited by the reduced friction of the ice, roller blading falls can range from slight abrasions to severe physical trauma. That is why it is most important through cross-training to increase the strength of the leg, thigh, and hip muscles for the purpose of maintaining muscle balance and coordination. Cross-training activities such as running sprints, swimming, and basketball can be important in maintaining overall aerobic endurance. Recommended flexibility exercises are the modified hurdler stretch, calf stretch, and lower-back stretch.

Cross-Training Activity Matrix

Key	Exercises	Strength	Muscular Endurance	Aerobic	Anaerobic	Warm-up/ Cool-down	Flexibility	Rehabilitation	Agility and Balance
T	Treadmill			○	○	○			
RM	Rowing Machine			○	○	○			
XC	X-C Ski Machine			○	○	○			
SM	StairMaster			○		○			
VC	Versa Climber		☆		☆	○			
B	Bicycling			☆	☆	☆			
S	Swimming			○			○		
AJ	Aqua Jogging			○				☆	
A	Aerobics			○			○		○
LS	Lateral Sports				○				○
WT	Weight Training	☆	☆					☆	
P	Plyometrics	○	○					○	
AE	Arm Ergometer			○	○	○		○	
RB	Roller Blading			☆	☆				☆
RJ	Rope Jumping			○	○	○			○
AG	Agility Exercises				○				○
F	Flexibility Exercises					○	○		
R	Running			○	○	○			

○ = Recommended   ☆ = Highly Recommended

In-Line and Speed Skating

Aerobic/Anaerobic Sample Training Programs

3–Days–a–Week								
Program	1	2	3	4	5	6	7	Focus
1		RB/SS*		R		RB/SS		LB
2		RB/SS		RM		RB/SS		UB
3		RB/SS		VC		RB/SS		UB/LB

5–Days–a–Week								
Program	1	2	3	4	5	6	7	Focus
1	RB/SS	RJ		RB		B	RB/SS	LB
2	RB/SS	XC		RB		VC	RB/SS	UB/LB
3	RB/SS	AE		RB		P	RB/SS	UB

7–Days–a–Week								
Program	1	2	3	4	5	6	7	Focus
1	RB/SS	B	RB/SS	SM	RB/SS	RM	RB/SS	LB
2	RB/SS	A	RB/SS	VC	RB/SS	RJ	RB/SS	UB/LB
3	RB/SS	VC	RB/SS	RM	RB/SS	AE	RB/SS	UB

*RB/SS = In-line or speed skating

Estimated Training Emphasis (percent)		
Aerobic	Anaerobic	Combination
10	70	20

Weight Training Exercises

3-DAYS-A-WEEK

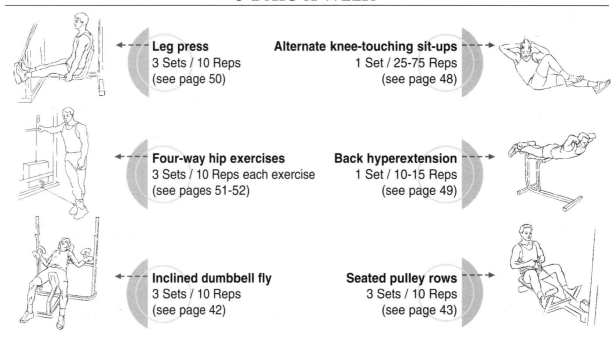

Leg press
3 Sets / 10 Reps
(see page 50)

Alternate knee-touching sit-ups
1 Set / 25-75 Reps
(see page 48)

Four-way hip exercises
3 Sets / 10 Reps each exercise
(see pages 51-52)

Back hyperextension
1 Set / 10-15 Reps
(see page 49)

Inclined dumbbell fly
3 Sets / 10 Reps
(see page 42)

Seated pulley rows
3 Sets / 10 Reps
(see page 43)

ADDITIONAL EXERCISES (OPTIONAL)

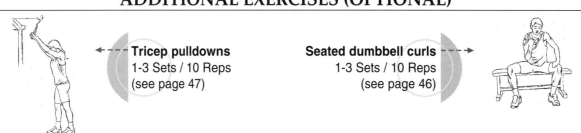

Tricep pulldowns
1-3 Sets / 10 Reps
(see page 47)

Seated dumbbell curls
1-3 Sets / 10 Reps
(see page 46)

In-Line and Speed Skating

Flexibility Exercises

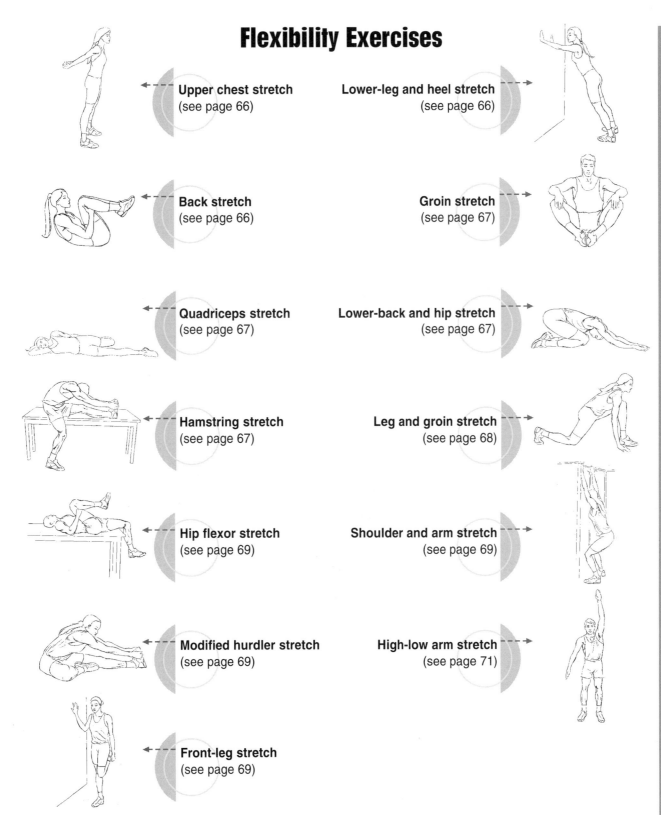

Upper chest stretch
(see page 66)

Lower-leg and heel stretch
(see page 66)

Back stretch
(see page 66)

Groin stretch
(see page 67)

Quadriceps stretch
(see page 67)

Lower-back and hip stretch
(see page 67)

Hamstring stretch
(see page 67)

Leg and groin stretch
(see page 68)

Hip flexor stretch
(see page 69)

Shoulder and arm stretch
(see page 69)

Modified hurdler stretch
(see page 69)

High-low arm stretch
(see page 71)

Front-leg stretch
(see page 69)

SPRINTING SPORTS PROGRAMS

Sprinting sports, unlike aerobic sports, rely predominantly on energy stored in the muscle and not the transport of oxygen by the cardiorespiratory system. Sprinting sports require the athlete to generate great amounts of force (anaerobic power) in a short period of time and require maximal efforts from 10 seconds up to 60 or 90 seconds in duration.

Sprint events such as track, cycling, and swimming are all characterized by intense muscular contractions that demand greater rates of energy production than can be provided by the aerobic system. Anaerobic power for sprinting requires the type of physical performance lying in the center of a continuum between strength and aerobic endurance. However, there is substantial overlap that occurs because the physiological boundaries are not precisely defined.

Because the muscles must withstand high-intensity activity for only a short period of time in sprinting sports, cross-training programs should include quick intervals of high-intensity activity along with lower-intensity types of exercise. Ideally, you should cross-train for sprint distances that are similar to those occurring in your sport so that the stress on the anaerobic systems are likewise similar.

It is important to vary the approach to sprint training so that boredom does not cause dropout from the sport. It is definitely worthwhile to perform an occasional training series of exercises that may not necessarily be ideal for improving anaerobic capacity, but is interesting and fun to perform nonetheless. Methods for improving sprint speeds may be classified into two categories: sprint-resisted and sprint-assisted training.

SPRINT-RESISTED EXERCISES

Sprinting is simulated with added resistance such as uphill running; weighted clothing; and swimming against the current, or in a tank, or against the strain gauge. The purpose here is to improve the dynamic strength factor by providing resistance through the range of movement and confronting the muscle with a greater overload than experienced in the specific sport. Some examples of cross-training for runners are pulling a weighted sled, running chutes, running uphill, running up steps, and plyometrics. Resistance training for swimmers may include wearing extra bathing suits, panty hose, towing buoys, and towing cables.

SPRINT-ASSISTED EXERCISES

Sprint-assisted training is a method where the purpose is to increase the speed of leg movement. Muscles required to contract more rapidly than during the regular activity can improve stride frequency (the number of steps in a given amount of time). Stride frequency improves the ability to decrease the time between strides while maintaining stride length. Cross-training methods for improving stride frequency include downhill running, towing behind an auto or other mechanical device at velocities above maximum, and treadmill running at supramaximal rates. Downhill running should be accomplished on three- to seven-degree slopes. Slopes more than seven degrees will result in an excessively fast stride frequency and may result in injury.

Additional methods of sprint training are programs that work on taking faster steps, longer steps, faster and longer steps, and on making quick accelerations to maximum speed. To develop proper form, the training should be at a slower speed (approximately 60-75 percent of maximum). When proper form has been developed, it may then be transformed to higher speeds.

Maximum effort training, or the use of high-intensity aerobic exercises that tax each individual to exhaustion, may also be used to produce psychological toughness, increase pain threshold, and improve psychological development beyond that from regular training. A cautionary note is that only those individuals with high levels of conditioning and motivation should incorporate this into their schedule. Some methods that are fairly popular are all-out sprints to exhaustion, one-legged distance hops for 90 seconds, running in place to exhaustion, two-legged hops for 45 seconds, and 300-yard sprints.

14

Sprint Running

Speed, strength, and power are all essential factors in sprinting success. Speed can be improved through the effective use of conditioning and the basic mechanics of running. Leg strength is vital not only for power off the blocks but for increasing stride length. By improving hip, leg, foot, and ankle strength, muscles will contract more swiftly and leg speed will be increased. Arm strength is also important as arm action contributes to sprint speed. Arm action has to be powerful, regular, and quick. Cross-training exercises such as plyometrics, weight training, and StairMaster are useful in increasing leg and arm strength and power.

Sprint running is basically a pushing and pulling action where the runner has the feeling of pushing the ground backward, then quickly pulling the leg forward to begin the push over again. Sprint-assisted running, such as running downhill at faster speeds than can be achieved on level surfaces can be a useful cross-training method. Requiring the legs to move faster without increases in stride distance has been shown to be effective in increasing leg speed during competitive sprinting. Assisted towing with a harness at faster speeds is also a great training tool. It's important to note that sprint-resistance running at slower speeds than those required in the activity has been shown to be ineffective in increasing propulsive force.

Cross-Training Activity Matrix

Sprint Running

Key	Exercises	Strength	Muscular Endurance	Aerobic	Anaerobic	Warm-up/Cool-down	Flexibility	Rehabilitation	Agility and Balance
T	Treadmill		○	○	☆				
RM	Rowing Machine		○	○	○				
XC	X-C Ski Machine			○					
SM	StairMaster			○					
VC	Versa Climber		○		☆				
B	Bicycling			○	☆	☆		○	
S	Swimming			○			○		
AJ	Aqua Jogging			○	○			☆	
A	Aerobics			○			○		○
LS	Lateral Sports				○				○
WT	Weight Training	☆	☆					☆	
P	Plyometrics	○	○					○	
AE	Arm Ergometer		○		☆				
RB	Roller Blading			○					○
RJ	Rope Jumping			○	○	○			
AG	Agility Exercises								○
F	Flexibility Exercises						○		

○ = Recommended   ☆ = Highly Recommended

Aerobic/Anaerobic Sample Training Programs

3–Days–a–Week								
Program	1	2	3	4	5	6	7	Focus
1		R*		XC		R		UB/LB
2		R		RM		R		UB
3		R		AJ		RB		LB

5–Days–a–Week								
Program	1	2	3	4	5	6	7	Focus
1	R	RM		R		S	R	UB
2	R	B		R		RB	R	LB
3	R	VC		R		XC	R	UB/LB

7–Days–a–Week								
Program	1	2	3	4	5	6	7	Focus
1	R	S	R	P	R	AE	R	UB
2	R	B	R	SM	R	AJ	R	LB
3	R	XC	R	RJ	R	VC	R	UB/LB

*R = Running

Estimated Training Emphasis (percent)			
Aerobic	Anaerobic	Combination	Competition Distance
	98	2	100-200 meters
5	80	15	400 meters

Weight Training Exercises

3-DAYS-A-WEEK

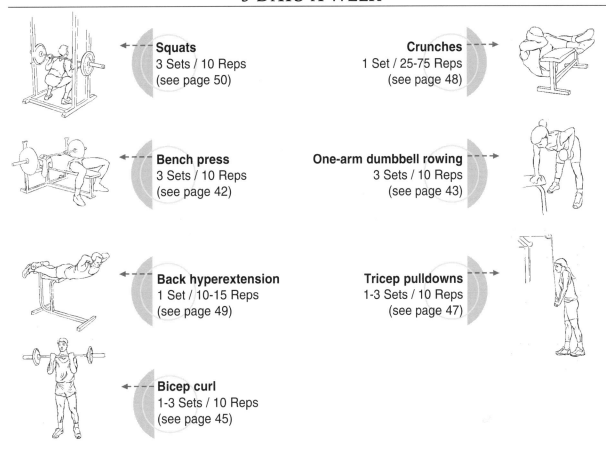

Squats
3 Sets / 10 Reps
(see page 50)

Crunches
1 Set / 25-75 Reps
(see page 48)

Bench press
3 Sets / 10 Reps
(see page 42)

One-arm dumbbell rowing
3 Sets / 10 Reps
(see page 43)

Back hyperextension
1 Set / 10-15 Reps
(see page 49)

Tricep pulldowns
1-3 Sets / 10 Reps
(see page 47)

Bicep curl
1-3 Sets / 10 Reps
(see page 45)

ADDITIONAL EXERCISES (OPTIONAL)

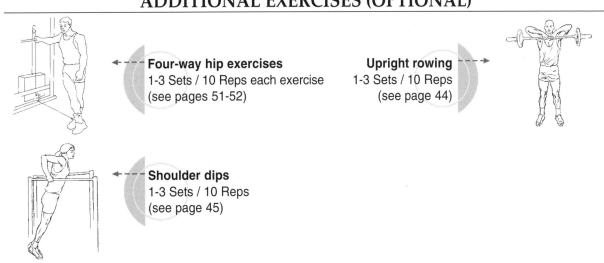

Four-way hip exercises
1-3 Sets / 10 Reps each exercise
(see pages 51-52)

Upright rowing
1-3 Sets / 10 Reps
(see page 44)

Shoulder dips
1-3 Sets / 10 Reps
(see page 45)

Flexibility Exercises

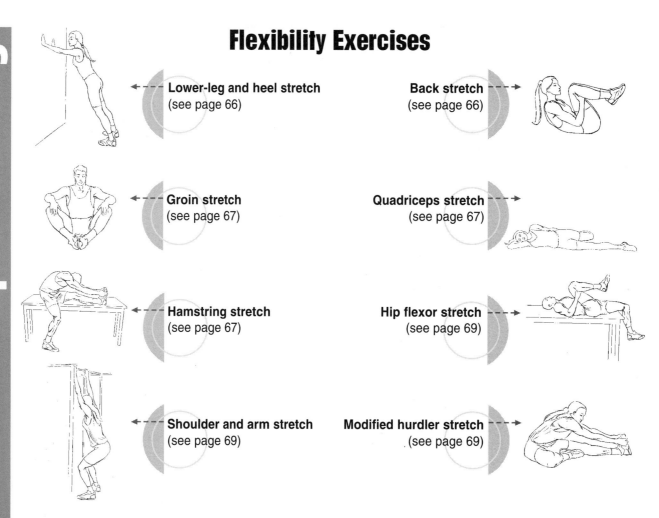

Lower-leg and heel stretch
(see page 66)

Back stretch
(see page 66)

Groin stretch
(see page 67)

Quadriceps stretch
(see page 67)

Hamstring stretch
(see page 67)

Hip flexor stretch
(see page 69)

Shoulder and arm stretch
(see page 69)

Modified hurdler stretch
(see page 69)

Sprint Cycling

Competitive sprint cycling places heavy demands on the physiological systems of the body. The neuromuscular system, especially the muscles and nerves of the legs, experience a great deal of stress as a result of the intensity of effort. The aerobic system is pushed to its maximal limit in a very short period of time so that the body is taxing primarily the anaerobic energy system in response. For the sprinter, the most important energy sources are the high-energy compounds stored in the muscles. Cross-training methods can significantly aid in the improvement of this energy system.

Sprint training regimens requiring the repetition of short sprints are the basis for primary-sport training programs. It is important to ride at maximum speed and all-out effort for 75 to 100 meters with relatively long rest periods in between rides. Cross-training methods used to increase strength are especially important for the quadriceps, hamstring, gluteal, calf, lower back, and shoulder muscles. Using plyometrics and resistance cords to increase strength will improve sprint speed. A stationary bike is an excellent method to maintain and increase strength and cardiorespiratory endurance during bad weather conditions.

Cross-Training Activity Matrix

Key	Exercises	Strength	Muscular Endurance	Aerobic	Anaerobic	Warm-up/Cool-down	Flexibility	Rehabilitation	Agility and Balance
T	Treadmill			O	O	O			
RM	Rowing Machine		O	O	O				
XC	X-C Ski Machine		O	O	O				
SM	StairMaster			O	O	O			
VC	Versa Climber		☆		☆				
S	Swimming			O			O		
AJ	Aqua Jogging			☆	O			☆	
A	Aerobics			O			O		O
LS	Lateral Sports				O				O
WT	Weight Lifting	☆	☆					O	
P	Plyometrics	O	O					O	
AE	Arm Ergometer		O	O	O			O	
RB	Roller Blading			O					O
RJ	Rope Jumping			O	O	O			
AG	Agility Exercises				O				O
F	Flexibility Exercises						O		
R	Running			O	O	O			

O = Recommended   ☆ = Highly Recommended

Aerobic/Anaerobic Sample Training Programs

3–Days–a–Week								
Program	1	2	3	4	5	6	7	Focus
1		B*		XC		B		UB/LB
2		B		RM		B		UB
3		B		R		B		LB

5–Days–a–Week								
Program	1	2	3	4	5	6	7	Focus
1	B	SM		B		RJ	B	LB
2	B	VC		B		A	B	UB/LB
3	B	RM		B		AE	B	UB

7–Days–a–Week								
Program	1	2	3	4	5	6	7	Focus
1	B	SM	B	RB	B	R	B	LB
2	B	VC	B	AJ	B	RJ	B	UB/LB
3	B	RM	B	S	B	AE	B	UB

*B = Cycling

Estimated Training Emphasis (percent)		
Aerobic	Anaerobic	Combination
	95	5

Weight Training Exercises

3-DAYS-A-WEEK

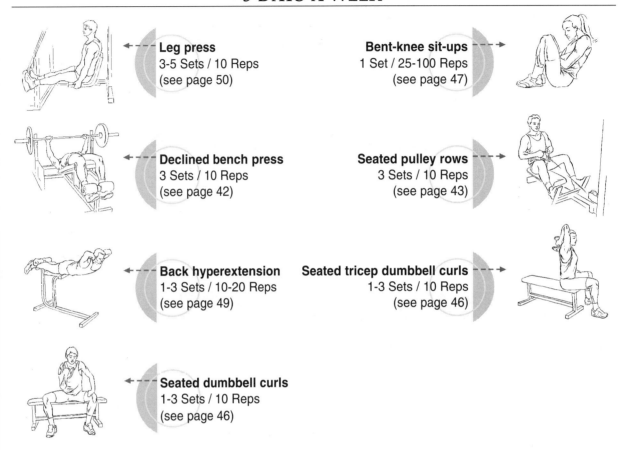

Leg press
3-5 Sets / 10 Reps
(see page 50)

Bent-knee sit-ups
1 Set / 25-100 Reps
(see page 47)

Declined bench press
3 Sets / 10 Reps
(see page 42)

Seated pulley rows
3 Sets / 10 Reps
(see page 43)

Back hyperextension
1-3 Sets / 10-20 Reps
(see page 49)

Seated tricep dumbbell curls
1-3 Sets / 10 Reps
(see page 46)

Seated dumbbell curls
1-3 Sets / 10 Reps
(see page 46)

ADDITIONAL EXERCISES (OPTIONAL)

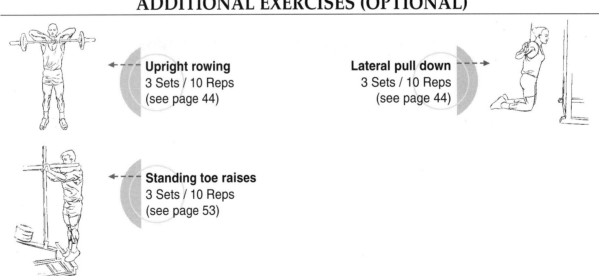

Upright rowing
3 Sets / 10 Reps
(see page 44)

Lateral pull down
3 Sets / 10 Reps
(see page 44)

Standing toe raises
3 Sets / 10 Reps
(see page 53)

Flexibility Exercises

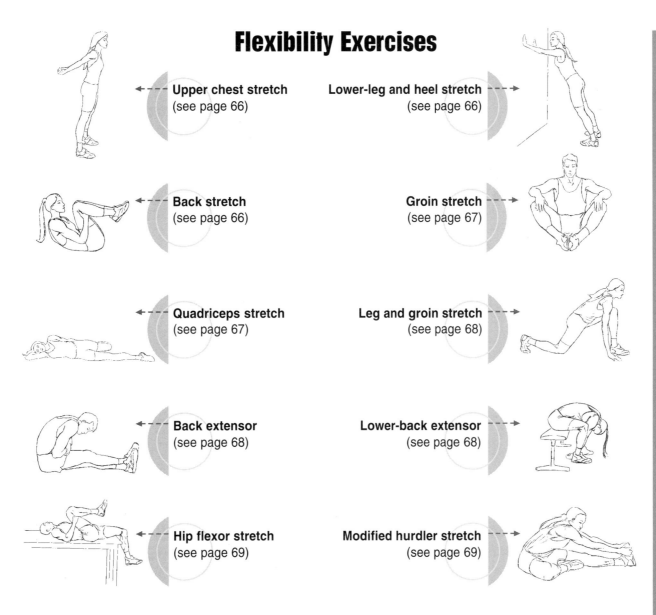

Upper chest stretch
(see page 66)

Lower-leg and heel stretch
(see page 66)

Back stretch
(see page 66)

Groin stretch
(see page 67)

Quadriceps stretch
(see page 67)

Leg and groin stretch
(see page 68)

Back extensor
(see page 68)

Lower-back extensor
(see page 68)

Hip flexor stretch
(see page 69)

Modified hurdler stretch
(see page 69)

16

Sprint Swimming

Sprint swimming, not unlike other anaerobic activities, requires a high degree of muscle strength and power, especially in the shoulder, hip, and leg muscles. Sprint swimming also depends primarily on the anaerobic energy systems to provide immediate energy for explosive power. In addition, good flexibility of the shoulder and hip muscles is vital.

Sprint swimming training requires repetition of short sprints by swimming at maximum speeds and all-out effort for 25 to 50 meters with relatively long rest periods between laps. This type of training will increase the amount of propulsive force by recruiting a greater number of fast-contracting muscle fibers that are physiologically equipped for anaerobic work. Also, short repeats at maximum speeds with short rests in between will increase the muscle stores of high-energy compounds and important enzymes essential in sprint swimming.

Cross-training should include activities such as land drills that require limb movements at fast speeds or speeds faster than low speeds in competition. Sprint-assisted training such as running downhill at speeds exceeding those that can be achieved on a level surface also aids in building leg strength. Sprint-assisted training by the use of towing can also be productive in increasing speed. When using these methods, be sure to follow the principles of specificity, overload, and progression as discussed in chapter 3. Conversely, sprint-resistant training at slower speeds than required in the sport tend not to increase propulsive force and speed.

Cross-Training Activity Matrix

Key	Exercises	Strength	Muscular Endurance	Aerobic	Anaerobic	Warm-up/ Cool-down	Flexibility	Rehabilitation	Agility and Balance
T	Treadmill			○	○	○			
RM	Rowing Machine		○	○	○	○			
XC	X-C Ski Machine			○	○	○			
SM	StairMaster			○		○			
VC	Versa Climber		○		☆				
B	Bicycling			○	○	☆			
AJ	Aqua Jogging			○	○			○	
A	Aerobics			○			○		○
LS	Lateral Sports				○				○
WT	Weight Training	☆	☆					☆	
P	Plyometrics	○	○					○	
AE	Arm Ergometer	○	☆		☆			☆	
RB	Roller Blading			○					○
RJ	Rope Jumping			○	○	○			
AG	Agility Exercises				○				○
F	Flexibility Exercises						○		
R	Running			○	○	○			

○ = Recommended   ☆ = Highly Recommended

Aerobic/Anaerobic Sample Training Programs

3–Days–a–Week							
Program	1	2	3	4	5	6	7	Focus
1		S*		VC		S		UB/LB
2		S		AE		S		UB
3		S		RB		S		LB

5–Days–a–Week							
Program	1	2	3	4	5	6	7	Focus
1	S	SM		S		R	S	LB
2	S	XC		S		A	S	UB/LB
3	S	RM		S		RJ	S	UB

7–Days–a–Week							
Program	1	2	3	4	5	6	7	Focus
1	S	SM	S	RB	S	B	S	LB
2	S	AE	S	RM	S	P	S	UB
3	S	XC	S	A	S	VC	S	UB/LB

*S = Swimming

Estimated Training Emphasis (percent)			
Aerobic	Anaerobic	Combination	Competition Distance
	98	2	50 meters
5	80	15	100 meters

Weight Training Exercises

3-DAYS-A-WEEK

FOR FREESTYLE, FLY, AND BACKSTROKE

Hip flexion
3 Sets / 10 Reps
(see page 51)

Hip extension
3 Sets / 10 Reps
(see page 51)

FOR BREAST STROKE AND MEDLEY

Hip abduction
3 Sets / 10 Reps
(see page 52)

Hip adduction
3 Set / 10 Reps
(see page 51)

FOR ALL STROKES

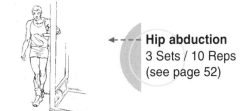
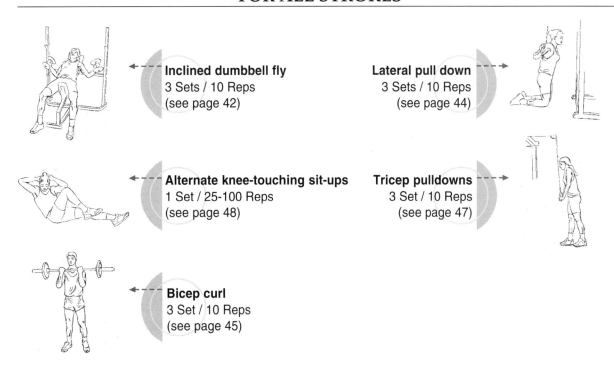

Inclined dumbbell fly
3 Sets / 10 Reps
(see page 42)

Lateral pull down
3 Sets / 10 Reps
(see page 44)

Alternate knee-touching sit-ups
1 Set / 25-100 Reps
(see page 48)

Tricep pulldowns
3 Set / 10 Reps
(see page 47)

Bicep curl
3 Set / 10 Reps
(see page 45)

Also utilize, if available, a swim bench (i.e., VASA swim bench) to practice the actual stroke mechanics with resistance.

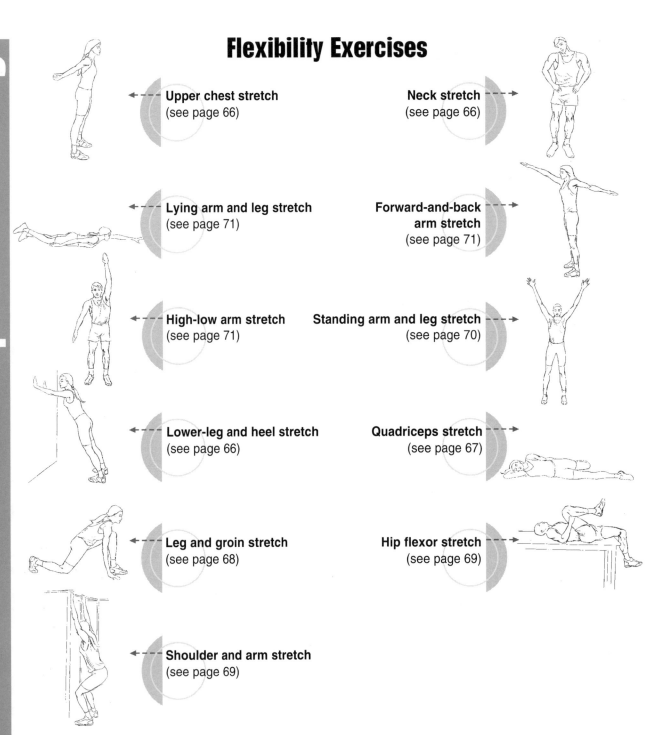

Flexibility Exercises

Upper chest stretch
(see page 66)

Neck stretch
(see page 66)

Lying arm and leg stretch
(see page 71)

Forward-and-back arm stretch
(see page 71)

High-low arm stretch
(see page 71)

Standing arm and leg stretch
(see page 70)

Lower-leg and heel stretch
(see page 66)

Quadriceps stretch
(see page 67)

Leg and groin stretch
(see page 68)

Hip flexor stretch
(see page 69)

Shoulder and arm stretch
(see page 69)

Sprint Swimming

Alpine Skiing

Skiing is primarily an anaerobic sport. The leg and thigh muscles involved in skiing perform high-intensity activity for only a short period of time. The cross-training program should mix quick, powerful bursts of activity with low-intensity types of exercise. It is important to work as many different muscle groups as possible through a variety of range of motion. Because downhill skiing is a high-risk sport, weight training is an important factor in reducing injury and developing muscle balance by strengthening all major muscle groups, with special emphasis on strengthening the quadriceps muscles to protect the knee.

Flexibility is especially important in skiing. Increased flexibility in the joints enables you to be more powerful and flowing. The ability to flex and extend your limbs lets you "spring load" them for more power and loosen them for increased absorption of bumps and dips in the terrain.

Cross-Training Activity Matrix

Alpine Skiing

Key	Exercises	Strength	Muscular Endurance	Aerobic	Anaerobic	Warm-up/ Cool-down	Flexibility	Rehabilitation	Agility and Balance
T	Treadmill			O	O				
RM	Rowing Machine		O		O				
XC	X-C Ski Machine			O	O				
SM	StairMaster			O	O	O			
VC	Versa Climber		O		O	O			
B	Bicycling			☆	O	☆		☆	
S	Swimming			O			O		
AJ	Aqua Jogging			O	O			O	
A	Aerobics			O			O		O
LS	Lateral Sports				O				O
WT	Weight Training	☆	☆					☆	
P	Plyometrics	O	O					O	
AE	Arm Ergometer		☆	O	O			O	
RB	Roller Blading			O	O				O
RJ	Rope Jumping			O		O			
AG	Agility Exercises								O
F	Flexibility Exercises						O		
R	Running			☆	O				

O = Recommended   ☆ = Highly Recommended

146

Aerobic/Anaerobic Sample Training Programs

Program	\multicolumn{8}{c}{3–Days–a–Week}

Program	1	2	3	4	5	6	7	Focus
1		SK*		B		SK		LB
2		SK		RM		SK		UB
3		SK		XC		SK		UB/LB

Program	1	2	3	4	5	6	7	Focus
\multicolumn{9}{c}{5–Days–a–Week}								
1	SK	SM		SK		RB	SK	LB
2	SK	A		SK		AG	SK	UB/LB
3	SK	VC		SK		RJ	SK	UB

Program	1	2	3	4	5	6	7	Focus
\multicolumn{9}{c}{7–Days–a–Week}								
1	SK	VC	SK	XC	SK	A	SK	UB/LB
2	SK	RM	SK	VC	SK	P	SK	UB
3	SK	SM	SK	B	SK	R	SK	LB

*SK = skiing

Estimated Training Emphasis (percent)		
Aerobic	Anaerobic	Combination
	80	20

Weight Training Exercises

3-DAYS-A-WEEK

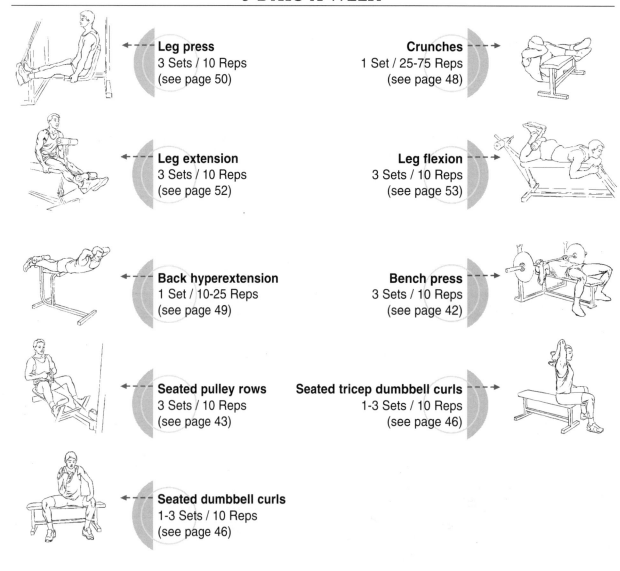

Leg press
3 Sets / 10 Reps
(see page 50)

Crunches
1 Set / 25-75 Reps
(see page 48)

Leg extension
3 Sets / 10 Reps
(see page 52)

Leg flexion
3 Sets / 10 Reps
(see page 53)

Back hyperextension
1 Set / 10-25 Reps
(see page 49)

Bench press
3 Sets / 10 Reps
(see page 42)

Seated pulley rows
3 Sets / 10 Reps
(see page 43)

Seated tricep dumbbell curls
1-3 Sets / 10 Reps
(see page 46)

Seated dumbbell curls
1-3 Sets / 10 Reps
(see page 46)

ADDITIONAL EXERCISES (OPTIONAL)

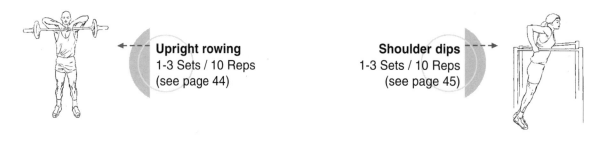

Upright rowing
1-3 Sets / 10 Reps
(see page 44)

Shoulder dips
1-3 Sets / 10 Reps
(see page 45)

Flexibility Exercises

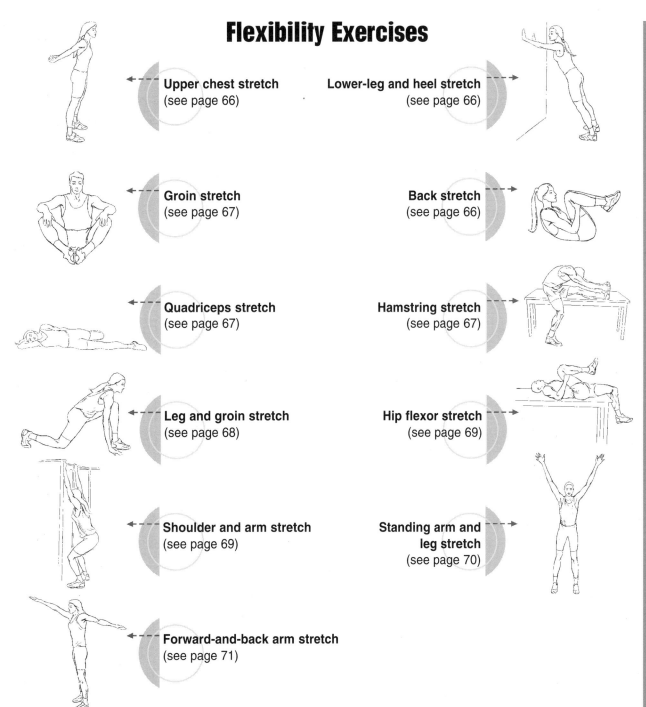

Upper chest stretch
(see page 66)

Lower-leg and heel stretch
(see page 66)

Groin stretch
(see page 67)

Back stretch
(see page 66)

Quadriceps stretch
(see page 67)

Hamstring stretch
(see page 67)

Leg and groin stretch
(see page 68)

Hip flexor stretch
(see page 69)

Shoulder and arm stretch
(see page 69)

Standing arm and
leg stretch
(see page 70)

Forward-and-back arm stretch
(see page 71)

Ice Hockey

Hockey requires strength, speed, finesse, and cardiorespiratory endurance. However, without endurance, strength, speed, and finesse are compromised. If your endurance is high, you can remain effective for each of the 20-minute play periods. Strength is a major factor in such skills as shooting, body checking, and strong skating strides. Hockey requires the use of many muscles necessary to perform at a great variety of angles and speeds. Muscle endurance allows the player to maintain these skills at peak level. Strength, endurance, and flexibility are crucial in enabling the player to quickly change direction, maintain position, and defend against the opposition. Increasing strength for the purpose of muscle balance—particularly in the leg, thigh, hip, lower back, shoulder, and chest muscles—is essential.

Recommended activities for training aerobic endurance include running, rope jumping, biking, stepups, and incline run-up stairs. Hurdle, calf, and lower-back stretches affect muscle groups used frequently in hockey. In addition, obstacle runs and zigzag running can better agility.

Cross-Training Activity Matrix

Key	Exercises	Strength	Muscular Endurance	Aerobic	Anaerobic	Warm-up/ Cool-down	Flexibility	Rehabilitation	Agility and Balance
T	Treadmill			O	O	O			
RM	Rowing Machine		O	O	O	O			
XC	X-C Ski Machine		O	O	O	O			
SM	StairMaster			O		O			
VC	Versa Climber		☆	O	☆	O			
B	Bicycling			☆	☆	☆			
S	Swimming			O			O	O	
AJ	Aqua Jogging			O				☆	
A	Aerobics			O			O		O
LS	Lateral Sports				O				O
WT	Weight Training	☆	☆					☆	
P	Plyometrics	O	O					O	
AE	Arm Ergometer		☆	O	O				
RB	Roller Blading			☆					☆
RJ	Rope Jumping			O	O	O			O
AG	Agility Exercises				O				O
F	Flexibility Exercises					O	O		
R	Running			O	O				

O = Recommended   ☆ = Highly Recommended

Aerobic/Anaerobic Sample Training Programs

3–Days–a–Week								
Program	1	2	3	4	5	6	7	Focus
1		SK*		R		SK		LB
2		SK		RM		SK		UB
3		SK		VC		SK		UB/LB

5–Days–a–Week								
Program	1	2	3	4	5	6	7	Focus
1	SK	RJ		SK		XC	SK	UB/LB
2	SK	SM		SK		B	SK	LB
3	SK	LS		SK		AE	SK	UB

7–Days–a–Week								
Program	1	2	3	4	5	6	7	Focus
1	SK	B	SK	RB	SK	R	SK	LB
2	SK	RJ	SK	VC	SK	XC	SK	UB/LB
3	SK	VC	SK	RM	SK	AE	SK	UB

*SK = Skating or hockey

Estimated Training Emphasis (percent)		
Aerobic	Anaerobic	Combination
	80	20

Weight Training Exercises

3-DAYS-A-WEEK

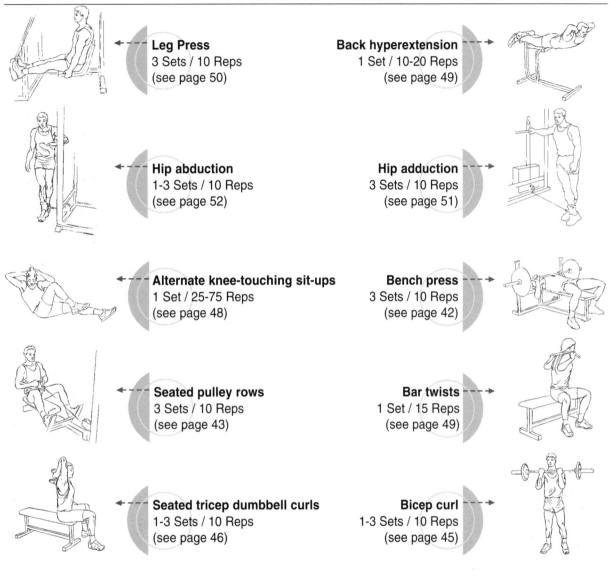

Leg Press
3 Sets / 10 Reps
(see page 50)

Back hyperextension
1 Set / 10-20 Reps
(see page 49)

Hip abduction
1-3 Sets / 10 Reps
(see page 52)

Hip adduction
3 Sets / 10 Reps
(see page 51)

Alternate knee-touching sit-ups
1 Set / 25-75 Reps
(see page 48)

Bench press
3 Sets / 10 Reps
(see page 42)

Seated pulley rows
3 Sets / 10 Reps
(see page 43)

Bar twists
1 Set / 15 Reps
(see page 49)

Seated tricep dumbbell curls
1-3 Sets / 10 Reps
(see page 46)

Bicep curl
1-3 Sets / 10 Reps
(see page 45)

ADDITIONAL EXERCISES (OPTIONAL)

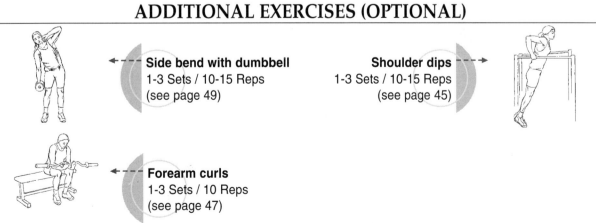

Side bend with dumbbell
1-3 Sets / 10-15 Reps
(see page 49)

Shoulder dips
1-3 Sets / 10-15 Reps
(see page 45)

Forearm curls
1-3 Sets / 10 Reps
(see page 47)

Flexibility Exercises

Upper chest stretch
(see page 66)

Lower-leg and heel stretch
(see page 66)

Back stretch
(see page 66)

Groin stretch
(see page 67)

Quadriceps stretch
(see page 67)

Lower-back and hip stretch
(see page 67)

Hamstring stretch
(see page 67)

Leg and groin stretch
(see page 68)

Hip flexor stretch
(see page 69)

Shoulder and arm stretch
(see page 69)

Modified hurdler stretch
(see page 69)

High-low arm stretch
(see page 71)

POWER SPORTS PROGRAMS

Power is the ability of muscles to produce high levels of force in a short time (explosive strength). To illustrate, say two individuals can lift 200 pounds a distance of four feet, but one can lift it faster than the other; in this case we say the one who lifts the weight faster has more power. Power is basically the product of strength and speed. By increasing either one, you can increase power. For instance, a discus thrower's power can be increased by improving his arm, shoulder girdle, and back strength, all muscles involved in the sport, or by improving the speed with which the movement is accomplished.

In many sports, power is more important than strength. The ability to block an opponent in football, put the shot, and high jump and long jump all require an element of power. In activities such as rebounding in basketball or the lateral movement of a football lineman, power combines a need for coordination and agility.

In field events such as jumping and vaulting, body weight becomes a factor. Optimal body weight will result in the greatest strength and speed combination. For example, if a jumper loses too much weight, strength may be reduced, but if the jumper gains too much weight, extra strength is of no value.

Weight training and other strength training methods are best for developing both strength and power because activities that develop strength also develop power. By increasing maximal power at a constant velocity, power will also be increased in an accelerating movement. For example, the vertical height for a high jumper may be increased by a constant-velocity leg press exercise, and lifting weights at slower speeds will help increase power in the faster movement of shot putting. While it is important to train at the same velocity as the sport's movement, one cannot lift weights at the velocities utilized in the shot put and adjustments must be made. Also, by increasing strength, muscles, tendons, and ligaments become stronger and less susceptible to injury. Strength training programs for power should consist of one to six repetition maximums in order to ensure increases in muscle strength.

Because training effects occur within the muscles, it is important to remember that certain conditioning in one activity does not necessarily carry over to another. When using an off-season training program that consists of strength training, flexibility exercises, and anaerobic activities, be certain that you combine your cross-training activities with specific drills and movements used in your sport.

As mentioned in chapters 3 and 4, plyometric exercises such as standing jumps, stadium hops (feet together up steps), ankle hops, and box-to-box jumping are extremely useful for increasing power, especially in sports that require repeated, rapid, vertical jumping such as basketball and volleyball. Plyometric cross-training activities for these kinds of sports should consist primarily of vertical jumps such as jumping over barriers or lateral hopping over cones.

19

Football

The sport of football has long used cross-training for its athletes. Football coaches were among the first to use strength training to enhance performance and universally use running to enhance cardiorespiratory endurance.

Demanding training sessions are important to avoid the fourth-quarter injuries that often result from poor conditioning. Strength training is a prime objective. Offensive and defensive linemen are required to have high levels of upper body and leg strength. Defensive backs also need upper body strength, flexibility, and rapid recovery from anaerobic activity. Running backs must have leg strength and power as well as upper body strength. Good flexibility is also important in preventing injury because of the stresses involuntarily placed on the joints during tackling and blocking.

Recommended cross-training activities for football include handball, basketball, soccer, paddle ball, speed ball, and jogging for aerobic and anaerobic endurance and weight training for strength and power. Please examine the cross-training matrix for other exercises that can add variety to your off-season and/or cross-training program.

Cross-Training Activity Matrix

Key	Exercises	Strength	Muscular Endurance	Aerobic	Anaerobic	Warm-up/Cool-down	Flexibility	Rehabilitation	Agility and Balance
T	Treadmill		O	O	O	O			
RM	Rowing Machine		O		O				
XC	X-C Ski Machine			O		O			
SM	StairMaster			O		O			
VC	Versa Climber		O		O				
B	Bicycling			O	☆	O		O	
S	Swimming			O			O		
AJ	Aqua Jogging			O				☆	
A	Aerobics		O	O			O		O
LS	Lateral Sports				O				O
WT	Weight Training	☆	☆					☆	
P	Plyometrics	O						O	
AE	Arm Ergometer		☆		☆			O	
RB	Roller Blading			O					O
RJ	Rope Jumping			O		O			
AG	Agility Exercises								O
F	Flexibility Exercises						O		
R	Running			O	☆	☆			

O = Recommended   ☆ = Highly Recommended

Aerobic/Anaerobic Sample Training Programs

Program	3–Days–a–Week							Focus
	1	2	3	4	5	6	7	
1		R*		SM		R		LB
2		R		AE		R		UB
3		R		RJ		R		UB/LB

Program	5–Days–a–Week							Focus
	1	2	3	4	5	6	7	
1	R	SM		R		RB	B	LB
2	R	VC		R		XC	B	UB/LB
3	R	AE		A		RM	B	UB/LB

Program	7–Days–a–Week							Focus
	1	2	3	4	5	6	7	
1	R	XC	RB	VC	SM	AE	B	UB/LB
2	R	RM	B	RJ	AE	VC	B	UB
3	R	B	RB	SM	AJ	LS	B	LB

*R = Running or football

Estimated Training Emphasis (percent)		
Aerobic	Anaerobic	Combination
	50	50

Weight Training Exercises

MON-WED-FRI

Bench press
3-5 Sets / 6-10 Reps
(see page 42)

One-arm dumbbell rowing
3-5 Sets / 1-10 Reps
(see page 43)

Crunches
1 Set / 25-75 Reps
(see page 48)

Military press
3 Sets / 8-10 Reps
(see page 44)

Lateral pull down
3 Sets / 8-10 Reps
(see page 44)

Back hyperextension
1 Set / 10-25 Reps
(see page 49)

Tricep pullovers
3 Sets / 8-12 Reps
(see page 47)

Bicep curl
3 Sets / 8-12 Reps
(see page 45)

TUE-THU-SAT

Squats
3 Sets / 8-12 Reps
(see page 50)

Incline bench sit-ups
1 Set / 15-50 Reps
(see page 48)

Leg extension
3 Sets / 10 Reps
(see page 52)

Leg flexion
3 Sets / 10 Reps
(see page 53)

ADDITIONAL EXERCISES

Side bend with dumbbell
1 Set / 15-25 Reps
(see page 49)

Forearm curls
1-3 Sets / 10-12 Reps
(see page 47)

Flexibility Exercises

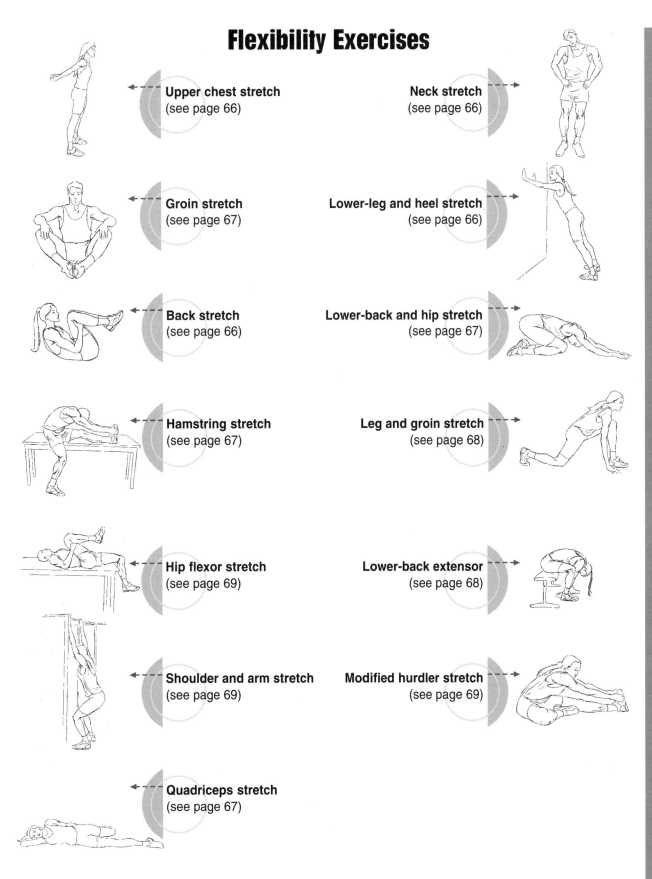

Upper chest stretch
(see page 66)

Neck stretch
(see page 66)

Groin stretch
(see page 67)

Lower-leg and heel stretch
(see page 66)

Back stretch
(see page 66)

Lower-back and hip stretch
(see page 67)

Hamstring stretch
(see page 67)

Leg and groin stretch
(see page 68)

Hip flexor stretch
(see page 69)

Lower-back extensor
(see page 68)

Shoulder and arm stretch
(see page 69)

Modified hurdler stretch
(see page 69)

Quadriceps stretch
(see page 67)

chapter

20

Field Events

Success in field events depends primarily

on muscle strength, speed, and power. For example, in field activities requiring jumping, the ability to thrust forcefully at takeoff demands great muscle strength. In distance jumping, the speed of the run at takeoff and the height of one's center of gravity from the ground are important. Cross-training activities should strengthen the abdominal, lower back, hip, and leg muscles. In addition to regular weight training, rope work and high-bar work are excellent for pole vaulters.

Weight events such as throwing require a smooth, well-coordinated execution of several closely related techniques combined with speed and exceptional strength. Throwing activities such as the shot, discus, and hammer require explosive power, rather than slow, deliberate strength. Weight training should concentrate on explosive moves such as found in Olympic lifts.

Recommended cross-training activities include obstacle courses involving climbing, jumping, swinging, and crawling. Relay games, soccer, tag games, running on trails or in intervals on the grass or beach can also be effective.

Cross-training activities such as arm ergometry, resistance cords, and Versa Climber are terrific for increasing muscle strength and endurance for field athletes. Plyometrics such as standing jumps, box jumping, and stadium hops (with both feet) are excellent cross-training methods for the jumping sports.

Cross Training Activity Matrix

Key	Exercises	Strength	Muscular Endurance	Aerobic	Anaerobic	Warm-up/Cool-down	Flexibility	Rehabilitation	Agility and Balance
T	Treadmill			○	○	○			
RM	Rowing Machine		○		○				
XC	X-C Ski Machine			○		○			
SM	StairMaster			○		○			
VC	Versa Climber		☆		☆				
B	Bicycling			○	☆	☆		☆	
S	Swimming			○			○		
AJ	Aqua Jogging			○				☆	
A	Aerobics			○			○		○
LS	Lateral Sports				○				○
WT	Weight Training	☆	☆					☆	
P	Plyometrics	☆						○	
AE	Arm Ergometer	○	☆		○				
RB	Roller Blading			○					
RJ	Rope Jumping			○					
AG	Agility Exercises				○				○
F	Flexibility Exercises						○		
R	Running			○	☆	○			

○ = Recommended ☆ = Highly Recommended

Field Events

Aerobic/Anaerobic Sample Training Programs

3–Days–a–Week							
Program	**1**	**2**	**3**	**4**	**5**	**6**	**7**	**Focus**
1		R*		SM		R		LB
2		R		VC		R		UB/LB
3		R		RM		R		UB

5–Days–a–Week							
Program	**1**	**2**	**3**	**4**	**5**	**6**	**7**	**Focus**
1	R	SM		R		B	R	LB
2	R	XC		R		LS	R	UB/LB
3	R	AE		R		P	R	UB

7–Days–a–Week							
Program	**1**	**2**	**3**	**4**	**5**	**6**	**7**	**Focus**
1	R	SM	R	B	R	AJ	R	LB
2	R	VC	R	RJ	R	A	R	UB/LB
3	R	AE	R	S	R	RM	R	UB

*R = Running or field events

Estimated Training Emphasis (percent)		
Aerobic	**Anaerobic**	**Combination**
	90	10

Weight Training Exercises

MON-WED-FRI

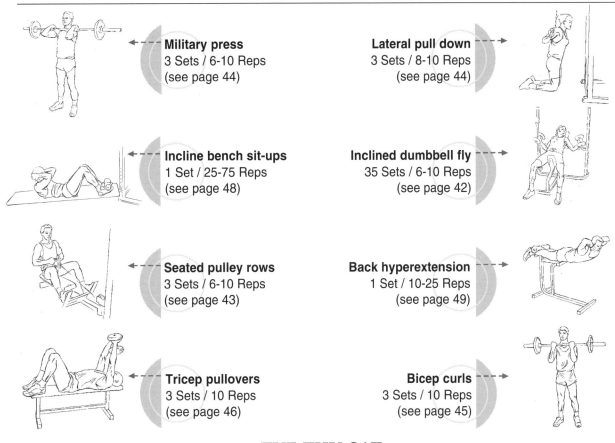

Military press
3 Sets / 6-10 Reps
(see page 44)

Lateral pull down
3 Sets / 8-10 Reps
(see page 44)

Incline bench sit-ups
1 Set / 25-75 Reps
(see page 48)

Inclined dumbbell fly
35 Sets / 6-10 Reps
(see page 42)

Seated pulley rows
3 Sets / 6-10 Reps
(see page 43)

Back hyperextension
1 Set / 10-25 Reps
(see page 49)

Tricep pullovers
3 Sets / 10 Reps
(see page 46)

Bicep curls
3 Sets / 10 Reps
(see page 45)

TUE-THU-SAT

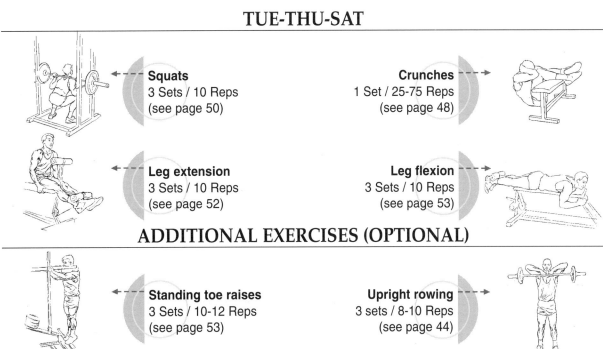

Squats
3 Sets / 10 Reps
(see page 50)

Crunches
1 Set / 25-75 Reps
(see page 48)

Leg extension
3 Sets / 10 Reps
(see page 52)

Leg flexion
3 Sets / 10 Reps
(see page 53)

ADDITIONAL EXERCISES (OPTIONAL)

Standing toe raises
3 Sets / 10-12 Reps
(see page 53)

Upright rowing
3 sets / 8-10 Reps
(see page 44)

Field Events

Bar Twists
3 Sets / 10-12 Reps
(see page 49)

Forearm curls
3 Sets / 10-12 Reps
(see page 47)

Side bend with dumbbell
3 Sets / 10-12 Reps
(see page 49)

Flexibility Exercises

Upper chest stretch
(see page 66)

Lower-leg and heel stretch
(see page 66)

Back stretch
(see page 66)

Groin stretch
(see page 67)

Quadriceps stretch
(see page 67)

Hamstring stretch
(see page 67)

Leg and groin stretch
(see page 68)

Back extensor
(see page 68)

Hip flexor stretch
(see page 69)

Front-leg stretch
(see page 69)

Shoulder and arm stretch
(see page 69)

Modified hurdler stretch
(see page 69)

166

Gymnastics

Gymnastics is not only a sport requiring strength, skill, and agility, but it is a form of art and self-expression as well. Although many of the basic skills in gymnastics are part of the conditioning process, there must be additional exercises to improve strength for all circumstances. Areas of importance are range of movement, strength and endurance, and postural and style training. All are important to prepare the body to perform skills efficiently and effectively. Training is also important to increase balance and reduce injuries; strength training should be used to correct specific weaknesses.

Specifically, the rings and parallel bars require high levels of arm and shoulder strength. Floor exercise, balance beam, and vaulting require a combination of muscle strength, balance, and agility.

Excellent activities for anaerobic endurance are rope jumping, circuit training, tennis, racquetball, and sprint running. Gymnasts also study ballet and work on body alignment and placement for agility and balance. Plyometrics, resistance cords, and weight training are important for strength and power. Flexibility exercises should be concentrated on the lower and upper back, groin, hamstrings, and trunk.

Cross-Training Activity Matrix

Key	Exercises	Strength	Muscular Endurance	Aerobic	Anaerobic	Warm-up/Cool-down	Flexibility	Rehabilitation	Agility and Balance
T	Treadmill			○	○	○			
RM	Rowing Machine		○	○	○				
XC	X-C Ski Machine			○	○				
SM	StairMaster			○		○			
VC	Versa Climber	☆		○	☆				
B	Bicycling			○	☆	☆			
S	Swimming			○			○		
AJ	Aqua Jogging			○				○	
A	Aerobics			○			○		○
LS	Lateral Sports				○				○
WT	Weight Training	☆	☆					☆	
P	Plyometrics	○	○					○	
AE	Arm Ergometer	○	☆		○	○		○	
RB	Roller Blading			○	○				○
RJ	Rope Jumping			○	○	○			
AG	Agility Exercises								☆
F	Flexibility Exercises					○	☆		
R	Running			○	○				

○ = Recommended   ☆ = Highly Recommended

Aerobic/Anaerobic Sample Training Programs

3–Days–a–Week								
Program	**1**	**2**	**3**	**4**	**5**	**6**	**7**	**Focus**
1		G*		AE		G		UB
2		G		RJ		G		UB/LB
3		G		SM		G		LB

5–Days–a–Week								
Program	**1**	**2**	**3**	**4**	**5**	**6**	**7**	**Focus**
1	G	LS		G		A	G	UB/LB
2	G	S		G		RM	G	UB
3	G	SM		G		B	G	LB

7–Days–a–Week								
Program	**1**	**2**	**3**	**4**	**5**	**6**	**7**	**Focus**
1	G	AE	G	VC	G	RM	G	UB
2	G	XC	G	A	G	RJ	G	UB/LB
3	G	B	G	SM	G	R	G	LB

*G = Gymnastics

Estimated Training Emphasis (percent)		
Aerobic	**Anaerobic**	**Combination**
	90	10

Gymnastics

169

Weight Training Exercises

3-DAYS-A-WEEK

Declined bench press
3 Sets / 10 Reps
(see page 42)

Lateral pull down
1 Set / 10 Reps
(see page 44)

Squats
3 Sets / 10 Reps
(see page 50)

Incline bench sit-ups
1 Set / 25-100 Reps
(see page 48)

Bicep curl
1-3 Sets / 10 Reps
(see page 45)

Shoulder dips
1-3 Set / 10-20 Reps
(see page 45)

ADDITIONAL EXERCISES (OPTIONAL)

Upright rowing (optional)
3 Sets / 10 Reps
(see page 44)

**Tricep pullovers
(optional)**
3 Sets / 10 Reps
(see page 46)

Flexibility Exercises

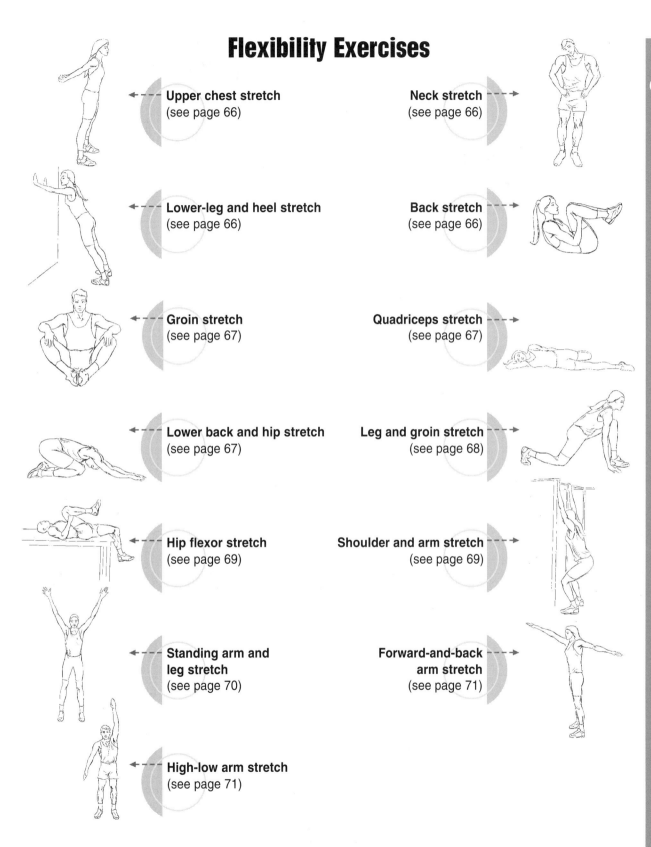

Upper chest stretch
(see page 66)

Neck stretch
(see page 66)

Lower-leg and heel stretch
(see page 66)

Back stretch
(see page 66)

Groin stretch
(see page 67)

Quadriceps stretch
(see page 67)

Lower back and hip stretch
(see page 67)

Leg and groin stretch
(see page 68)

Hip flexor stretch
(see page 69)

Shoulder and arm stretch
(see page 69)

**Standing arm and
leg stretch**
(see page 70)

**Forward-and-back
arm stretch**
(see page 71)

High-low arm stretch
(see page 71)

Weight and Power Lifting

chapter 22

To be good at Olympic-style or power lifts, you need to be able to exert a great amount of force in pulling and pushing movements. This activity places enormous demands on the shoulder muscles. Strong leg muscles are vital as well to maintain stability while lifting. The Olympic lifts, such as the press and snatch, also require speed and quickness. The power lifts—squat, dead lift, and bench press—do not require great speed for success, but as with the Olympic lifts, balance, coordination, and flexibility are needed. This chapter provides a simple introduction to training for weight and power lifting. We recommend that you consult additional material for more advanced training.

Integral to success in the styles of Olympic and power lifting is *periodization*, or using a different training focus to allow you to peak for a competition. A common type of periodization is as follows:

Phase 1—Hypertrophy: High reps (10-20) with heavier weights for 4 weeks.

Phase 2—Strength/power: Medium reps (5-8) with heavier weights for 4 weeks.

Phase 3—Peak phase: Few reps (2-3) with heavy weights for 3 weeks.

Phase 4—Active rest: Light, easy lifting and nonlifting activities such as cycling, running, and so forth.

Cross-training activities for weight and power lifting should be directed at aerobic work, such as rowing and StairMaster, and flexibility. The aerobic work will ease your recovery from workouts and enhance the length and quality of your workout. This type of work also provides a good warm-up and cool-down. Improvement in arm and shoulder flexibility can decrease post-workout soreness and may prevent injuries.

Cross-Training Activity Matrix

Key	Exercises	Strength	Muscular Endurance	Aerobic	Anaerobic	Warm-up/ Cool-down	Flexibility	Rehabilitation	Agility and Balance
T	Treadmill			○	○	○			
RM	Rowing Machine			○	○	○			
XC	X-C Ski Machine			○	○	○			
SM	StairMaster			○	○	○			
VC	Versa Climber		☆		☆	○			
B	Bicycling			☆	☆	☆			
S	Swimming			○			○		
AJ	Aqua Jogging			○			○	☆	
A	Aerobics			○		○	○		○
LS	Lateral Sports				○				○
WT	Weight Training	☆	☆					○	
P	Plyometrics	○	○					☆	
AE	Arm Ergometer		☆					○	
RB	Roller Blading			○	○	○			○
RJ	Rope Jumping			○	○	○			○
AG	Agility Exercises								○
F	Flexibility Exercises						○	○	
R	Running			○	○	○			

○ = Recommended   ☆ = Highly Recommended

Weight and Power Lifting

173

Aerobic/Anaerobic Sample Training Programs

3–Days–a–Week							
Program	1	2	3	4	5	6	7	Focus
1		L*		SM		L		LB
2		L		AE		L		UB
3		L		RJ		L		UB/LB

5–Days–a–Week							
Program	1	2	3	4	5	6	7	Focus
1	L	SM		L		B	L	LB
2	L	VC		L		XC	L	UB/LB
3	L	RM		L		P	L	UB

7–Days–a–Week							
Program	1	2	3	4	5	6	7	Focus
1	L	RB	L	R	L	B	L	LB
2	L	LS	L	XC	L	A	L	UB/LB
3	L	VC	L	AE	L	RM	L	UB

*L = Lifting

Estimated Training Emphasis (percent)		
Aerobic	Anaerobic	Combination
	98	2

Weight and Power Lifting

174

Weight Training Exercises

3-DAYS-A-WEEK

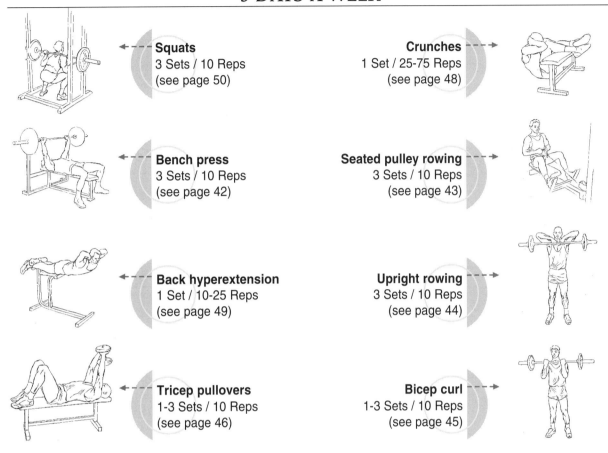

Squats
3 Sets / 10 Reps
(see page 50)

Crunches
1 Set / 25-75 Reps
(see page 48)

Bench press
3 Sets / 10 Reps
(see page 42)

Seated pulley rowing
3 Sets / 10 Reps
(see page 43)

Back hyperextension
1 Set / 10-25 Reps
(see page 49)

Upright rowing
3 Sets / 10 Reps
(see page 44)

Tricep pullovers
1-3 Sets / 10 Reps
(see page 46)

Bicep curl
1-3 Sets / 10 Reps
(see page 45)

EXERCISES FOR OLYMPIC-STYLE LIFTING (3-DAYS-A-WEEK)

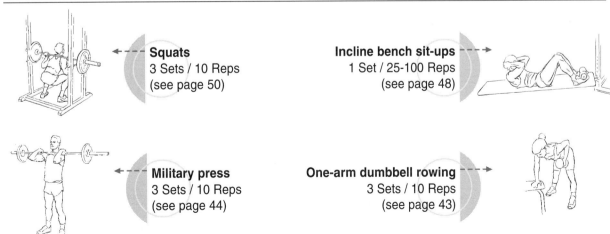

Squats
3 Sets / 10 Reps
(see page 50)

Incline bench sit-ups
1 Set / 25-100 Reps
(see page 48)

Military press
3 Sets / 10 Reps
(see page 44)

One-arm dumbbell rowing
3 Sets / 10 Reps
(see page 43)

Weight and Power Lifting

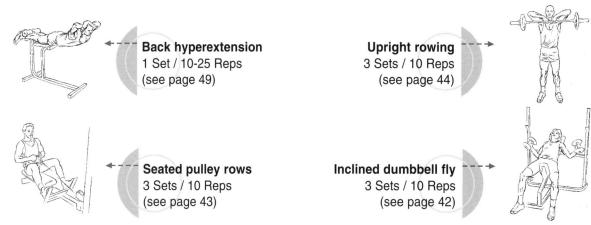

Back hyperextension
1 Set / 10-25 Reps
(see page 49)

Upright rowing
3 Sets / 10 Reps
(see page 44)

Seated pulley rows
3 Sets / 10 Reps
(see page 43)

Inclined dumbbell fly
3 Sets / 10 Reps
(see page 42)

After good levels of strength and muscular endurance are developed, then introduce and focus on the Olympic-style lift–press and snatch. For optimum development with these lifts, because of their technical nature, we suggest you consult a coach to assist you.

Flexibility Exercises

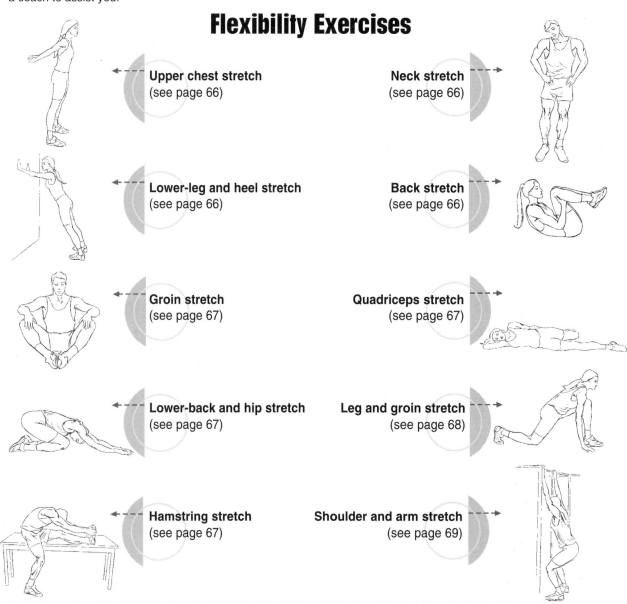

Upper chest stretch
(see page 66)

Neck stretch
(see page 66)

Lower-leg and heel stretch
(see page 66)

Back stretch
(see page 66)

Groin stretch
(see page 67)

Quadriceps stretch
(see page 67)

Lower-back and hip stretch
(see page 67)

Leg and groin stretch
(see page 68)

Hamstring stretch
(see page 67)

Shoulder and arm stretch
(see page 69)

Weight and Power Lifting

Wrestling

The sport of wrestling depends on a wide range of basic fundamental movements: dynamic movements such as jumping, crawling, running, and rolling; static movements (those done in place) such as lifting, pulling, pushing, bending, and twisting; and manipulative movements such as gripping and releasing. These basic movements all require a high level of muscle strength, especially arm and leg strength. Endurance, flexibility, and agility are also key components in wrestling. In addition, a lot of basic movements depend upon hip strength and power, and pulling movements depend upon biceps, forearms, and mid-back strength.

Cross-training provides a wide range of options for meeting the many demands of this sport. Cross-training activities for increasing strength include lifting drills, rope climbing, partner lifting, pulling and pushing opponents, and dumbbell swinging and plyometrics. Activities such as side jumping, bean walking (moving rapidly in all directions on hands and feet, belly down), and crab racing (same as bean walking but with your belly up) contribute to strength and agility. Continuous circling, rope jumping, and sprinting stimulate the anaerobic and aerobic energy systems.

Cross-Training Activity Matrix

Key	Exercises	Strength	Muscular Endurance	Aerobic	Anaerobic	Warm-up/ Cool-down	Flexibility	Rehabilitation	Agility and Balance
T	Treadmill			O	O	O			
RM	Rowing Machine		O	O	O	O			
XC	X-C Ski Machine		O	O	O	O			
SM	StairMaster			O		O			
VC	Versa Climber		☆	O	☆	O			
B	Bicycling			O	☆	☆		O	
S	Swimming			O			O		
AJ	Aqua Jogging			O				☆	
A	Aerobics			O			O		O
LS	Lateral Sports				O				O
WT	Weight Training	☆	☆					☆	
P	Plyometrics	O	O					O	
AE	Arm Ergometer			O				☆	
RB	Roller Blading			O					O
RJ	Rope Jumping			O	O				O
AG	Agility Exercises				O				O
F	Flexibility Exercises					O	O		
R	Running			☆	☆	O			

O = Recommended ☆ = Highly Recommended

Aerobic/Anaerobic Sample Training Programs

Program	1	2	3	4	5	6	7	Focus
3–Days–a–Week								
1		W*		B		W		LB
2		W		RM		W		UB
3		W		VC		W		UB/LB

Program	1	2	3	4	5	6	7	Focus
5–Days–a–Week								
1	W	RJ		W		XC	W	UB/LB
2	W	SM		W		R	W	LB
3	W	VC		W		S	W	UB

Program	1	2	3	4	5	6	7	Focus
7–Days–a–Week								
1	W	LS	W	VC	W	A	W	UB/LB
2	W	SM	W	RB	W	B	W	LB
3	W	AE	W	RM	W	P	W	UB

*W = Wrestling

Estimated Training Emphasis (percent)		
Aerobic	**Anaerobic**	**Combination**
	90	10

Weight Training Exercises

MON-WED-FRI

Squats
3 Sets / 10 Reps
(see page 50)

Standing toe raises
3 Sets / 10 Reps
(see page 53)

Crunches
1 Set / 25-75 Reps
(see page 48)

Back hyperextension
1 Set / 10-20 Reps
(see page 49)

Bar twists
1 Set / 10-15 Reps
(see page 49)

Side bend with dumbbell
1 Set / 10-15 Reps
(see page 49)

ADDITIONAL EXERCISES (OPTIONAL)

Leg extension
1-3 Sets / 10 Reps
(see page 52)

Leg flexion
1-3 Sets / 10 Reps
(see page 53)

TUE-THU-SAT

Bench press
3 Sets / 10 Reps
(see page 42)

Seated pulley rows
3 Sets / 10 Reps
(see page 43)

Alternate knee-touching sit-ups
1 Set / 25-75 Reps
(see page 48)

Triceps pullovers
3 Sets / 10 Reps
(see page 46)

Seated dumbbell curls
3 Sets / 10 Reps
(see page 46)

ADDITIONAL EXERCISES (OPTIONAL)

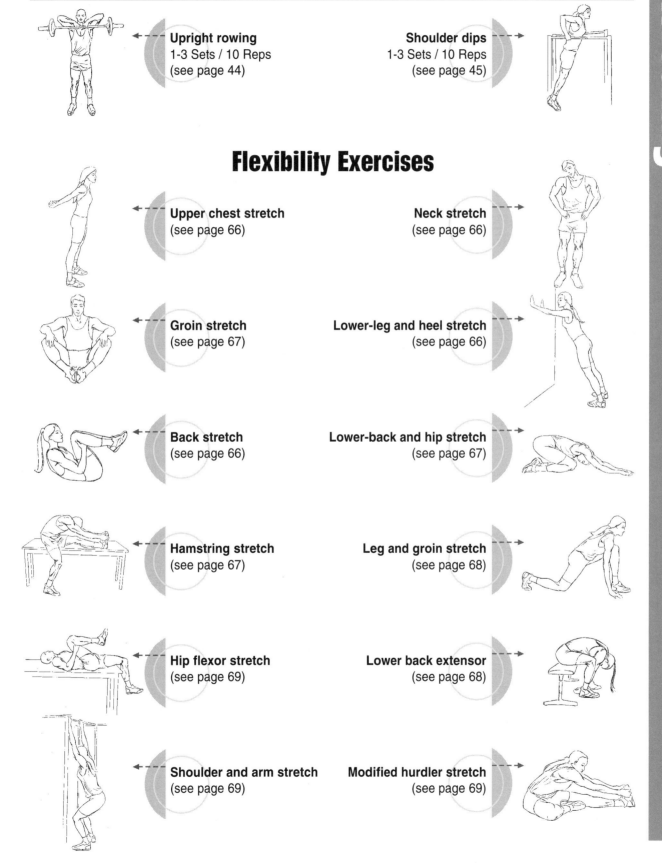

Upright rowing
1-3 Sets / 10 Reps
(see page 44)

Shoulder dips
1-3 Sets / 10 Reps
(see page 45)

Flexibility Exercises

Upper chest stretch
(see page 66)

Neck stretch
(see page 66)

Groin stretch
(see page 67)

Lower-leg and heel stretch
(see page 66)

Back stretch
(see page 66)

Lower-back and hip stretch
(see page 67)

Hamstring stretch
(see page 67)

Leg and groin stretch
(see page 68)

Hip flexor stretch
(see page 69)

Lower back extensor
(see page 68)

Shoulder and arm stretch
(see page 69)

Modified hurdler stretch
(see page 69)

chapter 24

Martial Arts

The martial arts—Karate, Tae Kwon Do, Judo, Jujitsu, Aikido, Kung Fu, Kempo, Hapkido, Tai Chi, Muay Thai, Jeet Kune Do, and other styles—place a premium on flexibility, speed, and power. Upper body strength is important, especially muscles in the arms, chest, and back for grabbing, pulling, punching, blocking, and throwing. Lower body strength is important for kicks, sweeps, and maintaining balance and strong stances. Agility is vital because of the variety of movements required in offense and defense.

Arm ergometry and weight training aid in building speed and power. Rowing, cross-country ski machines, Versa Climber, and cycling are excellent cross-training exercises for increasing endurance. Hip flexor, groin, and leg stretches are recommended as well. Flexibility exercises for the entire body are extremely important. Some exercises are shown here. However, additional exercises for specific needs should be included in your program. For example, Chinese splits can be a useful means to increasing the range of motion of the groin muscles.

Cross-Training Activity Matrix

Key	Exercises	Strength	Muscular Endurance	Aerobic	Anaerobic	Warm-up/ Cool-down	Flexibility	Rehabilitation	Agility and Balance
T	Treadmill			○	○	○			
RM	Rowing Machine		○	○	○	○			
XC	X-C Ski Machine		○	○	○	○			
SM	StairMaster			○		○			
VC	Versa Climber		☆		☆	○			
B	Bicycling			☆	☆	☆			
S	Swimming			○			○	○	
AJ	Aqua Jogging			○				☆	
A	Aerobics			○		○	○		○
LS	Lateral Sports				○				○
WT	Weight Training	☆	☆		○			☆	
P	Plyometrics	○	○					○	
AE	Arm Ergometer	○	☆		○			○	
RB	Roller Blading			○					○
RJ	Rope Jumping			○	○	○			○
AG	Agility Exercises				○				○
F	Flexibility Exercises					○	○	○	
R	Running			☆	☆	☆			

○ = Recommended   ☆ = Highly Recommended

Martial Arts

Aerobic/Anaerobic Sample Training Programs

3–Days–a–Week							
Program	**1**	**2**	**3**	**4**	**5**	**6**	**7**	**Focus**
1		MA*		B		MA		LB
2		MA		RM		MA		UB
3		MA		RJ		MA		UB/LB

5–Days–a–Week							
Program	**1**	**2**	**3**	**4**	**5**	**6**	**7**	**Focus**
1	MA	SM		MA		R	MA	LB
2	MA	S		MA		AE	MA	UB
3	MA	VC		MA		X-C	MA	UB/LB

7–Days–a–Week							
Program	**1**	**2**	**3**	**4**	**5**	**6**	**7**	**Focus**
1	MA	RJ	MA	X-C	MA	VC	MA	UB/LB
2	MA	SM	MA	R	MA	B	MA	LB
3	MA	AE	MA	P	MA	RM	MA	UB

*MA = Martial Arts

Estimated Training Emphasis (percent)		
Aerobic	**Anaerobic**	**Combination**
	90	10

184

Weight Training Exercises

3-DAYS-A-WEEK

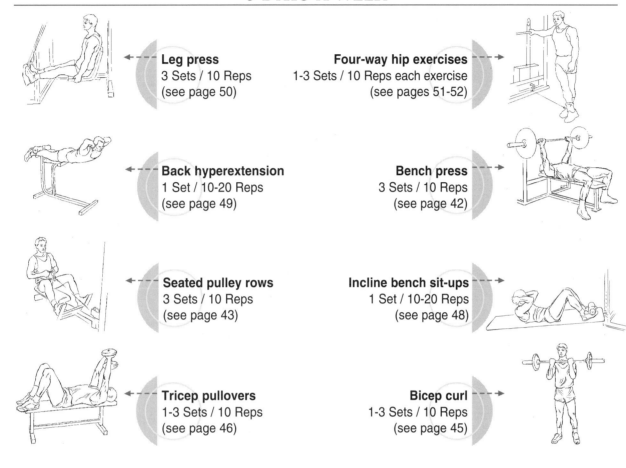

Leg press
3 Sets / 10 Reps
(see page 50)

Four-way hip exercises
1-3 Sets / 10 Reps each exercise
(see pages 51-52)

Back hyperextension
1 Set / 10-20 Reps
(see page 49)

Bench press
3 Sets / 10 Reps
(see page 42)

Seated pulley rows
3 Sets / 10 Reps
(see page 43)

Incline bench sit-ups
1 Set / 10-20 Reps
(see page 48)

Tricep pullovers
1-3 Sets / 10 Reps
(see page 46)

Bicep curl
1-3 Sets / 10 Reps
(see page 45)

ADDITIONAL EXERCISES (OPTIONAL)

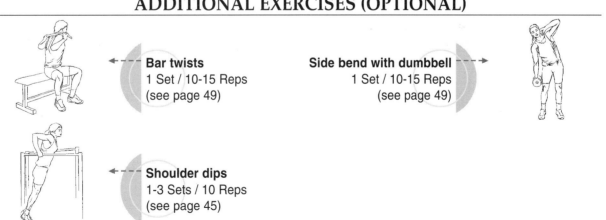

Bar twists
1 Set / 10-15 Reps
(see page 49)

Side bend with dumbbell
1 Set / 10-15 Reps
(see page 49)

Shoulder dips
1-3 Sets / 10 Reps
(see page 45)

Flexibility Exercises

Upper chest stretch
(see page 66)

Neck stretch
(see page 66)

Groin stretch
(see page 67)

Lower-leg and heel stretch
(see page 66)

Back stretch
(see page 66)

Lower-back and hip stretch
(see page 67)

Hamstring stretch
(see page 67)

Leg and groin stretch
(see page 68)

Hip flexor stretch
(see page 69)

Lower-back extensor
(see page 68)

Shoulder and arm stretch
(see page 69)

Modified hurdler stretch
(see page 69)

Martial Arts

Boxing

The sport of boxing places a premium on aerobic endurance, foot speed, and upper extremities power. Boxers were among the first athletes to cross-train, using running to increase their aerobic fitness. They traditionally have done abdominal work to strengthen their trunk muscles to better absorb the force of opponents' punches. Boxing also requires good balance and agility, especially in reacting to the opponents' punches.

The greatest change in training for boxers today is the addition of strength training to increase the boxer's punching power. This is accomplished by focusing the strength program on higher weights with fewer repetitions. In addition, plyometrics and resistance cords are excellent for building muscle strength and endurance.

Cross-Training Activity Matrix

Key	Exercises	Strength	Muscular Endurance	Aerobic	Anaerobic	Warm-up/ Cool-down	Flexibility	Rehabilitation	Agility and Balance
T	Treadmill			☆	☆	☆			
RM	Rowing Machine			○	○				
XC	X-C Ski Machine			○	○				
SM	StairMaster			○		☆			
VC	Versa Climber		☆	○	☆	○			
B	Bicycling			○	○	☆		○	
S	Swimming			○			○		
AJ	Aqua Jogging			○				☆	
A	Aerobics			○			○		○
LS	Lateral Sports				○				○
WT	Weight Training	☆	☆					☆	
P	Plyometrics	○	○					○	
AE	Arm Ergometer	○	☆		○				
RB	Roller Blading			○					○
RJ	Rope Jumping			☆	○	☆			○
AG	Agility Exercises				○				○
F	Flexibility Exercises					○	○		
R	Running			☆	☆	☆			

○ = Recommended   ☆ = Highly Recommended

Aerobic/Anaerobic Sample Training Programs

3–Days–a–Week								
Program	1	2	3	4	5	6	7	Focus
1		B*		AE		B		UB
2		B		SM		B		LB
3		B		VC		B		UB/LB

5–Days–a–Week								
Program	1	2	3	4	5	6	7	Focus
1	B	R		B		B	B	LB
2	B	S		B		AE	B	UB
3	B	VC		B		RJ	B	UB/LB

7–Days–a–Week								
Program	1	2	3	4	5	6	7	Focus
1	B	RJ	B	S	B	XC	B	UB/LB
2	B	SM	B	R	B	B	B	LB
3	B	AE	B	RM	B	P	B	UB

*B = Boxing

Estimated Training Emphasis (percent)		
Aerobic	Anaerobic	Combination
	90	10

Weight Training Exercises

3-DAYS-A-WEEK

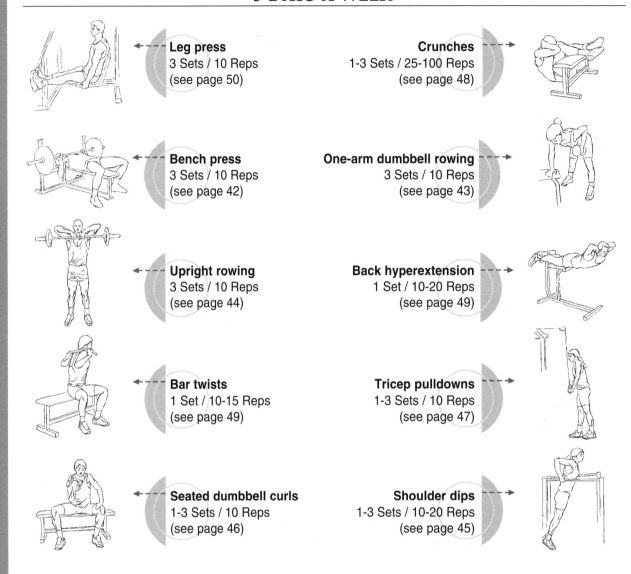

Leg press
3 Sets / 10 Reps
(see page 50)

Crunches
1-3 Sets / 25-100 Reps
(see page 48)

Bench press
3 Sets / 10 Reps
(see page 42)

One-arm dumbbell rowing
3 Sets / 10 Reps
(see page 43)

Upright rowing
3 Sets / 10 Reps
(see page 44)

Back hyperextension
1 Set / 10-20 Reps
(see page 49)

Bar twists
1 Set / 10-15 Reps
(see page 49)

Tricep pulldowns
1-3 Sets / 10 Reps
(see page 47)

Seated dumbbell curls
1-3 Sets / 10 Reps
(see page 46)

Shoulder dips
1-3 Sets / 10-20 Reps
(see page 45)

Flexibility Exercises

Upper chest stretch
(see page 66)

Neck stretch
(see page 66)

Groin stretch
(see page 67)

Lower-leg and heel stretch
(see page 66)

Back stretch
(see page 66)

Lower back and hip stretch
(see page 67)

Hamstring stretch
(see page 67)

Leg and groin stretch
(see page 68)

Hip flexor stretch
(see page 69)

Lower-back extensor
(see page 68)

Shoulder and arm stretch
(see page 69)

Modified hurdler stretch
(see page 69)

Shoulder stretch
(see page 71)

THROWING & STRIKING SPORTS PROGRAMS

Throwing and striking movements are an integral part of a number of physical activities including baseball, basketball, golf, volleyball, discus, javelin, badminton, and tennis.

Throwing and striking movements require a great deal of coordination and skill as well as the maximum speed of the distal limb segments. Therefore, to train the muscles for an overarm throw, it is vital to duplicate as closely as possible the speed and sequence of the movement of the arm muscles. To train the muscles effectively for this purpose, strength training must be performed at an accelerating rate. That is, the muscles must be trained by applying accelerating force from the beginning joint position throughout the range of movement.

Another important factor to consider is that at the end of throwing and striking movements the arm or leg begins to decelerate as a result of the braking action caused by the eccentric contraction of the antagonist muscle groups. (The antagonists are the muscles that act in opposition to the movement being done by the agonists, the muscles primarily responsible for creating a movement.) Therefore, it is also essential in strength training to decelerate the eccentric contraction of the antagonist muscle groups by means of a slow, negative contraction to protect them from injury during an abrupt decelerating movement and to strength train opposite muscle groups to ensure a strength balance.

Cross-training for strength should replicate as closely as possible the actual body movements of the sport's skill or activity. Strength training of the muscle groups that create the throwing and striking motion should be carried out using the exact plane, direction, range of joint movement, and speed of throwing and striking motion. Areas of concern are hip flexion, rotation of the shoulder, and flexion of the wrist—all of which play a major part in the nature of these dynamic skills. In addition, for activities requiring static strength (gymnastics, football, discus, weight lifting, and other sports that require holding starting positions), you should train for static strength in a position as close as possible to the actual performance.

For throwing heavy loads, training for strength at approximately the same speed as the throw itself is essential. The stronger the muscle group surrounding a particular muscle joint, the more easily the muscle groups can maintain angular velocity and longer radius of rotation resulting in greater acceleration.

THROWING AND STRIKING MOTIONS

Throwing and striking motions in the majority of sports may be divided into three phases: (1) a preparation phase that includes a static starting position or motion to place you into a starting position, such as the arm swing in the vertical jump; (2) an execution phase where you move to accomplish the mechanical aspects of the skill; and (3) a recovery or follow-through phase that includes the continuation of movement following execution of the skill used to achieve a balanced position or as preparation for the next movement (e.g., following through in pitching places the pitcher in a good position to field a batted ball).

The strength and endurance level of muscles are integral in these projection-type activities. For example, the extensor muscles play a major role in forcing the body from the ground. The muscles—such as in the hip, knee, and ankle—act as a spring when compressed. Simultaneous contraction of the antigravity muscles in the legs and hips provides the explosive power. The more gradual the deceleration, the less muscular force needed and the less danger of muscle strain on connective tissue. If eccentric contraction is not used, rapid movement can continue to the extreme end of the joint movement, producing sudden contact of joint structures and possible damage to bone cartilage and ligaments. The recovery phase of one skill may have to blend into the beginning phase of the next movement when a readiness position is required such as in racquet sports, volleyball, and fencing.

METHODS OF CROSS-TRAINING

Isokinetic exercises (see chapter 3) are effective in training for throwing and striking activities because one is able to duplicate speed and range of motion of overhand and underarm throws. Isokinetic exercise also permits the isolation of weak muscles, maximum resistance throughout the exercise range of motion, and quantification of torque work and power. Isokinetic exercise also provides a safety mechanism since there are no free weights to drop or lift.

Plyometric exercise is an effective way to blend speed and strength training. Plyometrics train you to start quicker, change direction more rapidly, accelerate faster, and improve overall strength. See chapter 4 for plyometric and other types of whole-body activities that promote agility and balance especially important to throwing and striking athletes.

Volleyball

The game of volleyball requires the player to use her body efficiently in creating, directing, and producing force: maximum force to serve the ball, controlled force to pass to a teammate, and minimum force to deceive an opponent by lightly tapping the ball over the net. The game demands a high level of strength, endurance, and flexibility.

Weight training goals are to increase strength, power, and explosiveness of the upper and lower body. Because of the continuous jumping, emphasis should also be placed on the lower body for muscle power.

Cross-training activities such as weight training with low repetition maximum at high intensity and plyometric exercises such as box jumping, two-foot ankle hop, split squat jumps, and lateral box jumping are important in building upper body strength and leg power.

Cross-training activities for aerobic endurance should include aqua jogging, StairMaster, circuit training, and treadmill running. Rapid cycling, sprint running, and Versa Climber are useful for stimulating the anaerobic energy system.

Cross-Training Activity Matrix

Volleyball

Key	Exercises	Strength	Muscular Endurance	Aerobic	Anaerobic	Warm-up/Cool-down	Flexibility	Rehabilitation	Agility and Balance
T	Treadmill			○	○	○			
RM	Rowing Machine		○	○	○	○			
XC	X-C Ski Machine			○	○	○			
SM	StairMaster			○		○			
VC	Versa Climber	☆		○	☆	○			
B	Bicycling			☆	☆	☆			
S	Swimming			○			○		
AJ	Aqua Jogging			○				☆	
A	Aerobics			○			○		○
LS	Lateral Sports				○				○
WT	Weight Training	☆	☆					☆	
P	Plyometrics	☆	☆					○	
AE	Arm Ergometer		○		○				
RB	Roller Blading			○					○
RJ	Rope Jumping			○					○
AG	Agility Exercises								○
F	Flexibility Exercises					○	○		
R	Running			☆	☆	☆			

○ = Recommended ☆ = Highly Recommended

Aerobic/Anaerobic Sample Training Programs

3–Days–a–Week							
Program	1	2	3	4	5	6	7	Focus
1		V*		AE		V		UB
2		V		VC		V		UB/LB
3		V		SM		V		LB

5–Days–a–Week							
Program	1	2	3	4	5	6	7	Focus
1	V	RM		V		S	V	UB
2	V	RJ		V		XC	V	UB/LB
3	V	R		V		B	V	LB

7–Days–a–Week							
Program	1	2	3	4	5	6	7	Focus
1	V	RJ	V	A	V	LS	V	UB/LB
2	V	R	V	RB	V	B	V	LB
3	V	RM	V	P	V	AE	V	UB

*V = Volleyball

Estimated Training Emphasis (percent)		
Aerobic	Anaerobic	Combination
	90	10

Weight Training Exercises

3-DAYS-A-WEEK

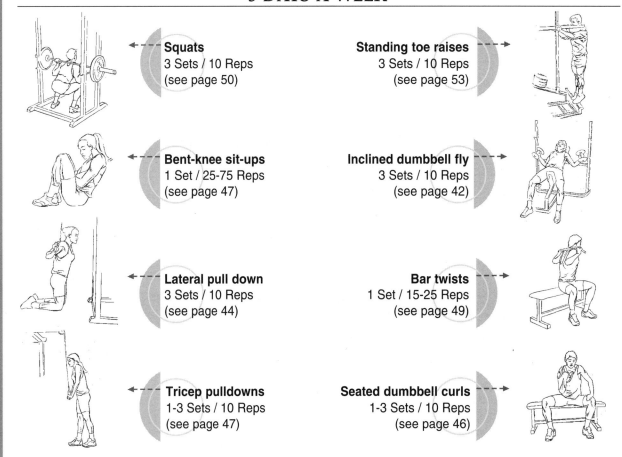

Squats
3 Sets / 10 Reps
(see page 50)

Standing toe raises
3 Sets / 10 Reps
(see page 53)

Bent-knee sit-ups
1 Set / 25-75 Reps
(see page 47)

Inclined dumbbell fly
3 Sets / 10 Reps
(see page 42)

Lateral pull down
3 Sets / 10 Reps
(see page 44)

Bar twists
1 Set / 15-25 Reps
(see page 49)

Tricep pulldowns
1-3 Sets / 10 Reps
(see page 47)

Seated dumbbell curls
1-3 Sets / 10 Reps
(see page 46)

Flexibility Exercises

Upper chest stretch
(see page 66)

Neck stretch
(see page 66)

Lower-leg and heel stretch
(see page 66)

Groin stretch
(see page 67)

Quadriceps stretch
(see page 67)

Leg and groin stretch
(see page 68)

Shoulder and arm stretch
(see page 69)

Shoulder stretch
(see page 71)

**Standing arm and
leg stretch**
(see page 70)

**Forward-and-back
arm stretch**
(see page 71)

High-low arm stretch
(see page 71)

Volleyball

27

Basketball

Basketball requires muscle strength for speed and rebounding and places heavy demands on the aerobic energy system. The conditioning program must exhaust the body beyond the fatigue level in order to prepare one to maintain high levels of skill when confronted with physical exertion and fatigue. Conditioning is also necessary to lessen the risk of injury when fatigue reduces a player's speed and agility.

Conditioning exercises must include stopping, starting, changing direction, jumping, and moving backwards. Cross-training activities such as tennis, handball, weight training, rope climbing, and passing and catching a medicine ball are useful in strengthening the hand, wrist, arm, and shoulder muscles. Weight training should emphasize both strength and endurance.

Plyometric exercises such as jumping over cones, feet-together rim jumps, lateral cone jumps, jumping from box to rim, depth jumps, and turning 180 degrees while jumping from a box are extremely useful activities for building leg power.

Cycling, running, and StairMaster workouts are also effective for increasing endurance.

Cross-Training Activity Matrix

Basketball

Key	Exercises	Strength	Muscular Endurance	Aerobic	Anaerobic	Warm-up/Cool-Down	Flexibility	Rehabilitation	Agility and Balance
T	Treadmill			◯		◯			
RM	Rowing Machine		◯	◯	◯				
XC	X-C Ski Machine			◯		◯			
SM	StairMaster			◯		◯			
VC	Versa Climber		◯		☆				
B	Bicycling			☆	☆	☆		◯	
S	Swimming			◯			◯	◯	
AJ	Aqua Jogging			◯				◯	
A	Aerobics			◯			◯		◯
LS	Lateral Sports				◯				◯
WT	Weight Training	☆	☆					◯	
P	Plyometrics	☆	☆					◯	
AE	Arm Ergometer		◯		◯			◯	
RB	Roller Blading			◯					◯
RJ	Rope Jumping			◯	◯	◯			◯
AG	Agility Exercises								☆
F	Flexibility Exercises						☆		
R	Running			☆	☆	☆			

◯ = Recommended   ☆ = Highly Recommended

201

Aerobic/Anaerobic Sample Training Programs

Program	1	2	3	4	5	6	7	Focus
				3–Days–a–Week				
1		R*		AE		R		UB
2		R		VC		R		UB/LB
3		R		SM		R		LB

Program	1	2	3	4	5	6	7	Focus
				5–Days–a–Week				
1	R	AE		R		RM	R	UB/LB
2	R	VC		R		RJ	R	UB/LB
3	R	SM		R		B	R	LB

Program	1	2	3	4	5	6	7	Focus
				7–Days–a–Week				
1	R	AE	R	RM	R	VC	R	UB/LB
2	R	B	R	RB	R	SM	R	LB
3	R	RJ	R	XC	R	A	R	UB/LB

*R = Running or basketball

Estimated Training Emphasis (percent)		
Aerobic	Anaerobic	Combination
	85	15

Weight Training Exercises

3-DAYS-A-WEEK

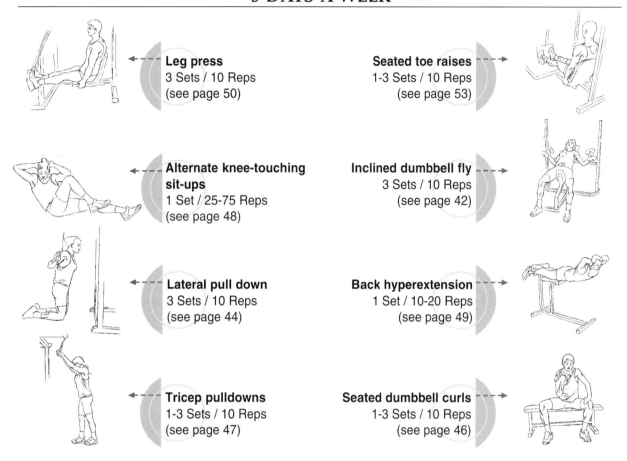

←--- **Leg press**
3 Sets / 10 Reps
(see page 50)

Seated toe raises ---→
1-3 Sets / 10 Reps
(see page 53)

←--- **Alternate knee-touching sit-ups**
1 Set / 25-75 Reps
(see page 48)

Inclined dumbbell fly ---→
3 Sets / 10 Reps
(see page 42)

←--- **Lateral pull down**
3 Sets / 10 Reps
(see page 44)

Back hyperextension ---→
1 Set / 10-20 Reps
(see page 49)

←--- **Tricep pulldowns**
1-3 Sets / 10 Reps
(see page 47)

Seated dumbbell curls ---→
1-3 Sets / 10 Reps
(see page 46)

Flexibility Exercises

Upper chest stretch
(see page 66)

Neck stretch
(see page 66)

Lower-leg and heel stretch
(see page 66)

Groin stretch
(see page 67)

Quadriceps stretch
(see page 67)

Leg and groin stretch
(see page 68)

Shoulder and arm stretch
(see page 69)

Shoulder stretch
(see page 71)

Standing arm and leg stretch
(see page 70)

**Forward-and-back
arm stretch**
(see page 71)

High-low arm stretch
(see page 71)

Baseball

most every phase of baseball requires a
degree of strength and flexibility. Pitchers are required to have
gh level of cardiorespiratory endurance, lower body strength,
bility, and shoulder and arm strength. Catchers must have leg
ngth, flexibility, agility, hand and wrist strength, and abdominal
ngth. Fielders require hand and wrist strength, upper body
ngth, and general flexibility.

ecause baseball requires only moderate levels of aerobic endur-
e, your training program should be weighted toward the anaero-
energy system. Important cross-training activities for anaerobic
durance are sprint running, sprint cycling, and workouts on the
rsa Climber. Tennis and racquetball are excellent for flexibility in
dition to anaerobic training.

Cross-Training Activity Matrix

Key	Exercises	Strength	Muscular Endurance	Aerobic	Anaerobic	Warm-up/ Cool-down	Flexibility	Rehabilitation	Agility and Balance
T	Treadmill			◖	◖	◖			
RM	Rowing Machine		◖	◖	◖	◖			
XC	X-C Ski Machine		◖	◖	◖	◖			
SM	StairMaster			◖		◖			
VC	Versa Climber		☆		☆				
B	Bicycling			☆	☆	☆			
S	Swimming			◖			◖		
AJ	Aqua Jogging			◖				☆	
A	Aerobics			◖			◖		◖
LS	Lateral Sports				◖				◖
WT	Weight Training	☆	☆					☆	
P	Plyometrics	◖	◖					◖	
AE	Arm Ergometer		◖		◖			◖	
RB	Roller Blading			◖					◖
RJ	Rope Jumping			◖		◖			
AG	Agility Exercises				◖				☆
F	Flexibility Exercises					◖	☆		
R	Running			◖	☆	☆			

◖ = Recommended   ☆ = Highly Recommended

Aerobic/Anaerobic Sample Training Programs

3–Days–a–Week								
Program	1	2	3	4	5	6	7	Focus
1		R*		RB		B		LB
2		RM		S		AE		UB
3		RJ		XC		VC		UB/LB

5–Days–a–Week								
Program	1	2	3	4	5	6	7	Focus
1	R	B		RB		SM	B	LB
2	R	AE		S		VC	RM	UB
3	R	VC		RJ		XC	SM	UB/LB

7–Days–a–Week								
Program	1	2	3	4	5	6	7	Focus
1	R	AJ	B	SM	LS	RB	AG	LB
2	RM	P	AE	XC	P	VC	S	UB
3	R	S	B	VC	SM	A	R	UB/LB

*R = Running or baseball

Estimated Training Emphasis (percent)		
Aerobic	Anaerobic	Combination
	80	20

Weight Training Exercises

3-DAYS-A-WEEK

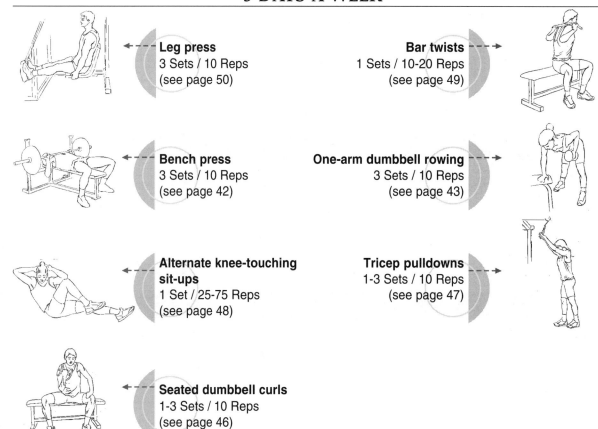

Leg press
3 Sets / 10 Reps
(see page 50)

Bar twists
1 Sets / 10-20 Reps
(see page 49)

Bench press
3 Sets / 10 Reps
(see page 42)

One-arm dumbbell rowing
3 Sets / 10 Reps
(see page 43)

Alternate knee-touching sit-ups
1 Set / 25-75 Reps
(see page 48)

Tricep pulldowns
1-3 Sets / 10 Reps
(see page 47)

Seated dumbbell curls
1-3 Sets / 10 Reps
(see page 46)

Flexibility Exercises

Upper chest stretch
(see page 66)

Lower-leg and heel stretch
(see page 66)

Back stretch
(see page 66)

Groin stretch
(see page 67)

Quadriceps stretch
(see page 67)

Leg and groin stretch
(see page 68)

Hip flexor stretch
(see page 69)

Shoulder and arm stretch
(see page 69)

Standing arm and leg stretch
(see page 70)

Forward-and-back arm stretch
(see page 71)

High-low arm stretch
(see page 71)

Shoulder stretch
(see page 71)

Baseball

29

Tennis

Tennis is a physically demanding game when played competitively and requires a great deal of conditioning. Tennis, like a number of sports, requires not only an appropriate diet, adequate rest periods, and a good mental attitude but also exercises designed to develop muscle strength and endurance, agility, flexibility, balance, speed, and coordination. It is important that the exercises approximate the demands of the actual competition. Important elements in developing a peak performance are maintaining a high level of fitness, motivation, and strength to prevent injuries. Tennis is a game of controlled force and form.

Cross-training activities should include stretching and agility drills, especially forward and lateral running. Tennis players also work on finger push-ups and finger flips to increase grip strength. Abdominal curl-ups are especially important in order to maintain strong abdominal muscles to protect the lower back from stressful lateral movements. Plyometrics such as medicine ball throwing, side-to-side ankle hops, standing jumps, and cone hops (lateral to front) are also useful for building strength and agility. Short sprints, rope jumping, circuit training, and distance running are recommended to stimulate the anaerobic and aerobic systems.

Cross-Training Activity Matrix

Key	Exercises	Strength	Muscular Endurance	Aerobic	Anaerobic	Warm-up/ Cool-down	Flexibility	Rehabilitation	Agility and Balance
T	Treadmill			○	○	○			
RM	Rowing Machine		○	○	○	○			
XC	X-C Ski Machine			○	○	○			
SM	StairMaster			○		○			
VC	Versa Climber		☆		☆				
B	Bicycling			☆	☆	☆			
S	Swimming			○			○		
AJ	Aqua Jogging			○				○	
A	Aerobics			○			○		○
LS	Lateral Sports				○				○
WT	Weight Training	☆	☆					☆	
P	Plyometrics	○	○					○	
AE	Arm Ergometer		○		○			○	
RB	Roller Blading			○					○
RJ	Rope Jumping			○	○	○			○
AG	Agility Exercises				○				☆
F	Flexibility Exercises					○	☆		
R	Running			☆	☆	☆			

○ = Recommended   ☆ = Highly Recommended

Aerobic/Anaerobic Sample Training Programs

| Program | 3–Days–a–Week | | | | | | | Focus |
	1	2	3	4	5	6	7	
1		T*		AG		T		LB
2		T		S		T		UB
3		T		RJ		T		UB/LB

| Program | 5–Days–a–Week | | | | | | | Focus |
	1	2	3	4	5	6	7	
1	T	SM		T		B	T	LB
2	T	AE		T		P	T	UB
3	T	XC		T		VC	T	UB/LB

| Program | 7–Days–a–Week | | | | | | | Focus |
	1	2	3	4	5	6	7	
1	T	SM	T	AG	T	R	T	LB
2	T	RM	T	VC	T	AE	T	UB
3	T	RJ	T	A	T	S	T	UB/LB

*T = Tennis

Estimated Training Emphasis (percent)		
Aerobic	Anaerobic	Combination
10	70	20

212

Weight Training Exercises

3-DAYS-A-WEEK

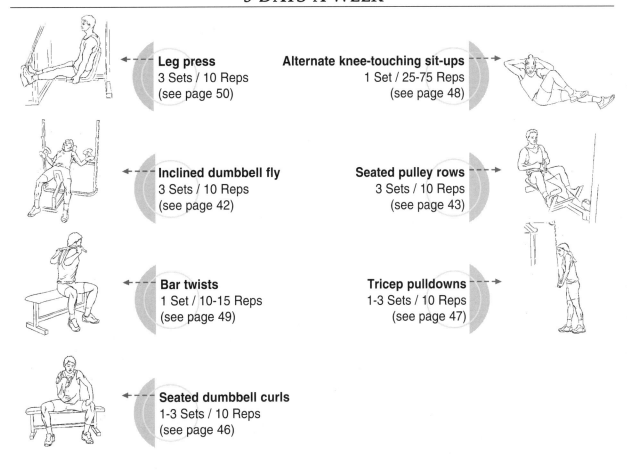

Leg press
3 Sets / 10 Reps
(see page 50)

Alternate knee-touching sit-ups
1 Set / 25-75 Reps
(see page 48)

Inclined dumbbell fly
3 Sets / 10 Reps
(see page 42)

Seated pulley rows
3 Sets / 10 Reps
(see page 43)

Bar twists
1 Set / 10-15 Reps
(see page 49)

Tricep pulldowns
1-3 Sets / 10 Reps
(see page 47)

Seated dumbbell curls
1-3 Sets / 10 Reps
(see page 46)

ADDITIONAL EXERCISES (OPTIONAL)

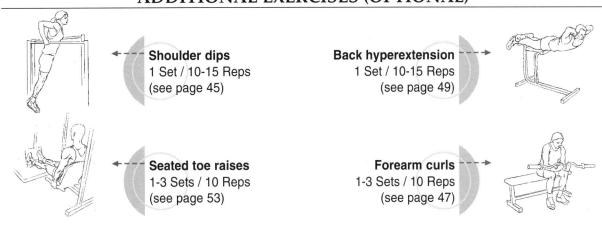

Shoulder dips
1 Set / 10-15 Reps
(see page 45)

Back hyperextension
1 Set / 10-15 Reps
(see page 49)

Seated toe raises
1-3 Sets / 10 Reps
(see page 53)

Forearm curls
1-3 Sets / 10 Reps
(see page 47)

Flexibility Exercises

Upper chest stretch
(see page 66)

Lower-leg and heel stretch
(see page 66)

Back stretch
(see page 66)

Groin stretch
(see page 67)

Quadriceps stretch
(see page 67)

Hamstring stretch
(see page 67)

Leg and groin stretch
(see page 68)

Shoulder and arm stretch
(see page 69)

Wall lean and heel stretch
(see page 70)

**Standing arm and
leg stretch**
(see page 70)

**Foreward-and-back
arm stretch**
(see page 71)

High-low arm stretch
(see page 71)

Golf

A golf swing can be analyzed to the point

that the competency would confuse most individuals. An educated golf swing is nevertheless the basis for the game. Each player must build a swing that is unique to his own body and try to make it as perfect as possible to reach a desired target.

Weight training can be used to increase strength and endurance, particularly to enhance trunk rotation and rotary movements as well as arm and leg strength. Good flexibility is also crucial in developing a coordinated golf swing and preventing lower back problems. Strong abdominal muscles are important to prevent lower back problems as well.

Even though golf does not demand a high level of aerobic energy, it is important to maintain moderate levels so that heavy breathing, after walking 300 yards up a hill, will not interfere with the fine muscle control needed to strike the ball or putt.

Running, cycling, Versa Climber workouts, and swimming are excellent activities for golfers who wish to maintain aerobic endurance.

Cross-Training Activity Matrix

Key	Exercises	Strength	Muscular Endurance	Aerobic	Anaerobic	Warm-up/ Cool-down	Flexibility	Rehabilitation	Agility and Balance
T	Treadmill			○	○	○			
RM	Rowing Machine			○	○	○			
XC	X-C Ski Machine			○	○	○			
SM	StairMaster			○		○			
VC	Versa Climber		☆		☆	○			
B	Bicycling			☆	☆	☆			
S	Swimming			○		○			
AJ	Aqua Jogging			○				☆	
A	Aerobics			○		○			○
LS	Lateral Sports				○				○
WT	Weight Training	☆	☆					☆	
P	Plyometrics	○	○					○	
AE	Arm Ergometer		○	○	○			○	
RB	Roller Blading			○					○
RJ	Rope Jumping			○	○	○			○
AG	Agility Exercises				○				☆
F	Flexibility Exercises					○	☆		
R	Running			☆	☆	☆			

○ = Recommended   ☆ = Highly Recommended

Aerobic/Anaerobic Sample Training Programs

Program	1	2	3	4	5	6	7	Focus
3–Days–a–Week								
1		G*		B		G		LB
2		G		RM		G		UB
3		G		RJ		G		UB/LB

Program	1	2	3	4	5	6	7	Focus
5–Days–a–Week								
1	G	R		G		SM	G	LB
2	G	AE		G		S	G	UB
3	G	A		G		XC	G	UB/LB

Program	1	2	3	4	5	6	7	Focus
7–Days–a–Week								
1	G	B	G	RB	G	SM	G	LB
2	G	RM	G	P	G	S	G	UB
3	G	VC	G	A	G	XC	G	UB/LB

*G = golf

Estimated Training Emphasis (percent)		
Aerobic	**Anaerobic**	**Combination**
	95	5

Weight Training Exercises

3 DAYS-A-WEEK

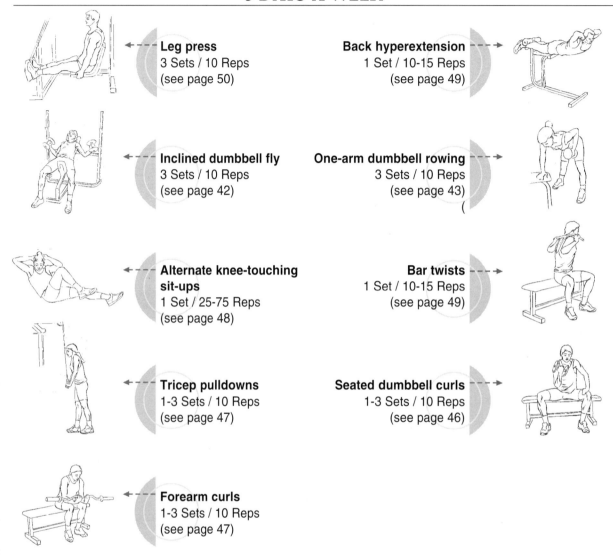

Leg press
3 Sets / 10 Reps
(see page 50)

Back hyperextension
1 Set / 10-15 Reps
(see page 49)

Inclined dumbbell fly
3 Sets / 10 Reps
(see page 42)

One-arm dumbbell rowing
3 Sets / 10 Reps
(see page 43)

Alternate knee-touching sit-ups
1 Set / 25-75 Reps
(see page 48)

Bar twists
1 Set / 10-15 Reps
(see page 49)

Tricep pulldowns
1-3 Sets / 10 Reps
(see page 47)

Seated dumbbell curls
1-3 Sets / 10 Reps
(see page 46)

Forearm curls
1-3 Sets / 10 Reps
(see page 47)

Flexibility Exercises

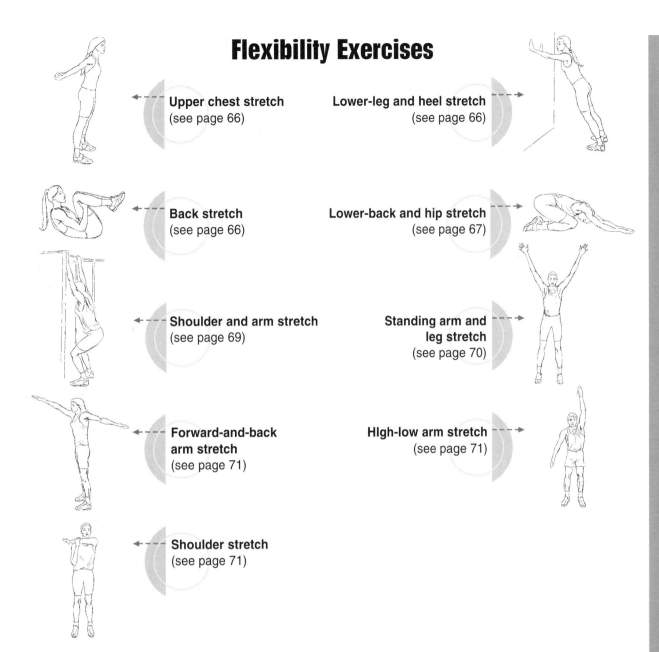

Upper chest stretch
(see page 66)

Lower-leg and heel stretch
(see page 66)

Back stretch
(see page 66)

Lower-back and hip stretch
(see page 67)

Shoulder and arm stretch
(see page 69)

**Standing arm and
leg stretch**
(see page 70)

**Forward-and-back
arm stretch**
(see page 71)

High-low arm stretch
(see page 71)

Shoulder stretch
(see page 71)

Racquetball, Handball, and Squash

Racquetball, handball, and squash are fast games that demand a great deal of strength and endurance, especially in the legs, as well as skill and body control. It has been estimated that a player may sprint approximately 1.5 miles in an average racquetball game. The ability to control the center of gravity is a key factor; therefore, strength training of the leg muscles is of paramount importance. Racquetball, handball, and squash work out nearly every part of the body. These court games also place heavy demands on the aerobic system. Cross-training can be useful in increasing muscle strength and endurance and also improving both the anaerobic and aerobic energy systems.

Cross-training exercises such as Versa Climber workouts, weight training, and arm ergometry are useful in building arm and grip strength. Plyometrics such as side-to-side ankle hops, box jumping, cone hops, and standing long jumps are excellent for building and maintaining leg strength.

Cycling, StairMaster, and rope jumping are only a few of the exercises listed in the matrix that are useful for building endurance. The emphasis should be mainly on the anaerobic energy system in these sports.

Cross-Training Activity Matrix

Key	Exercises	Strength	Muscular Endurance	Aerobic	Anaerobic	Warm-up/Cool-down	Flexibility	Rehabilitation	Agility and Balance
T	Treadmill			○	○	○			
RM	Rowing Machine	○		○	○	○			
XC	X-C Ski Machine			○	○	○			
SM	StairMaster			○		○			
VC	Versa Climber	○	○		○	○			
B	Bicycling			☆	☆	☆			
S	Swimming			○			○		
AJ	Aqua Jogging			○				○	
A	Aerobics			○			○		○
LS	Lateral Sports				○				○
WT	Weight Training	☆	☆					☆	
P	Plyometrics	○	○					○	
AE	Arm Ergometer	○	○		○			○	
RB	Roller Blading			○					○
RJ	Rope Jumping			○	○	○			○
AG	Agility Exercises				○				☆
F	Flexibility Exercises					○	☆		
R	Running			☆	☆	☆			

○ = Recommended   ☆ = Highly Recommended

Aerobic/Anaerobic Sample Training Programs

3–Days–a–Week							
Program	1	2	3	4	5	6	7	Focus
1		RHS*		RM		RHS		UB
2		RHS		B		RHS		LB
3		RHS		RJ		RHS		UB/LB

5–Days–a–Week							
Program	1	2	3	4	5	6	7	Focus
1	RHS	AE		RHS		S	RHS	UB
2	RHS	VC		RHS		XC	RHS	UB/LB
3	RHS	SM		RHS		B	RHS	LB

7–Days–a–Week							
Program	1	2	3	4	5	6	7	Focus
1	RHS	SM	RHS	B	RHS	RB	RHS	LB
2	RHS	RM	RHS	S	RHS	AE	RHS	UB
3	RHS	RJ	RHS	VC	RHS	A	RHS	UB/LB

*RHS = Racquetball, handball, squash

Estimated Training Emphasis (percent)		
Aerobic	Anaerobic	Combination
10	70	20

222

Weight Training Exercises

3-DAYS-A-WEEK

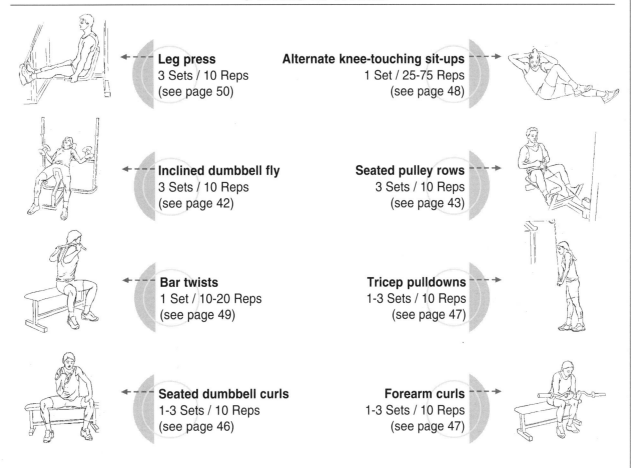

Leg press
3 Sets / 10 Reps
(see page 50)

Alternate knee-touching sit-ups
1 Set / 25-75 Reps
(see page 48)

Inclined dumbbell fly
3 Sets / 10 Reps
(see page 42)

Seated pulley rows
3 Sets / 10 Reps
(see page 43)

Bar twists
1 Set / 10-20 Reps
(see page 49)

Tricep pulldowns
1-3 Sets / 10 Reps
(see page 47)

Seated dumbbell curls
1-3 Sets / 10 Reps
(see page 46)

Forearm curls
1-3 Sets / 10 Reps
(see page 47)

ADDITIONAL EXERCISES

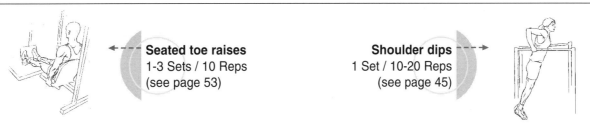

Seated toe raises
1-3 Sets / 10 Reps
(see page 53)

Shoulder dips
1 Set / 10-20 Reps
(see page 45)

Racquetball, Handball, and Squash

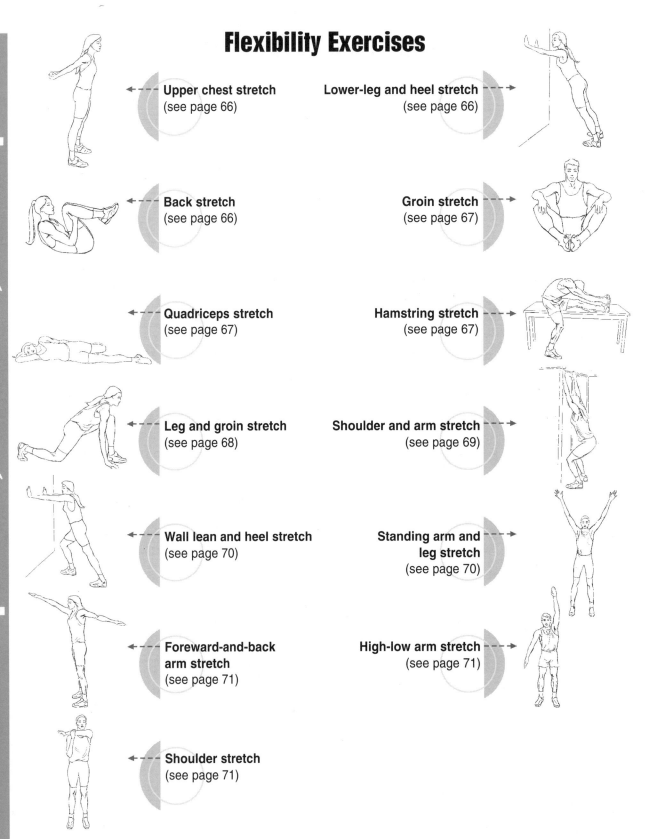

Flexibility Exercises

Upper chest stretch
(see page 66)

Lower-leg and heel stretch
(see page 66)

Back stretch
(see page 66)

Groin stretch
(see page 67)

Quadriceps stretch
(see page 67)

Hamstring stretch
(see page 67)

Leg and groin stretch
(see page 68)

Shoulder and arm stretch
(see page 69)

Wall lean and heel stretch
(see page 70)

**Standing arm and
leg stretch**
(see page 70)

**Foreward-and-back
arm stretch**
(see page 71)

High-low arm stretch
(see page 71)

Shoulder stretch
(see page 71)

Programs for Multisport Athletes

Previous chapters have focused on using cross-training methods, exercises, activities, and sports to improve your performance; rehabilitate, train through, or prevent injuries; and provide for psychological enhancement in a primary sport. This book would not be complete, however, without mentioning that many high school, college, and even adult athletes regularly participate in multiple, compatible sports for a variety of reasons. The purpose of this chapter is to acquaint you with important cross-training considerations should you decide to participate in two or more sports during the same year.

Some of the benefits of compatible multisport participation include

1. enhancing or maintaining primary-sport performance through the use of compatible energy systems;
2. promoting and maintaining all-around general physical fitness, which provides a base of support for multisport participation;
3. enhancing or maintaining primary-sport performance through the use of compatible muscle systems;
4. developing muscle coordination, agility, and skill building that promote all-around athletic performance;
5. providing a break from your primary sport to avoid boredom or overtraining;
6. the ability to participate in a fitness activity when participating in the primary sport is not possible due to a lack of essential components: snow, water, basic facilities, or other seasonal schedule concerns; and
7. providing training extension that cannot be done in the primary sport due to the risk of overtraining or overuse injury.

MULTISPORT COMPATIBILITY AND TRAINING

There are some unique challenges regarding type and intensity of training if you participate in two or more sports concurrently or during the same year. Some sports activities may be physically compatible, in that both require aerobic endurance such as distance running and distance swimming. Other sports may not be physically compatible because they make different training demands on the athlete. For example, tennis requires muscle power, agility, and fast reaction time, none of which are essential in distance running.

Competing in two or more sports also requires very high levels of fitness, especially if one or more of the sports requires aerobic endurance such as cross-country skiing or long-distance running. Athletes competing concurrently in duathlons or triathlons (swimming, biking, and running) have to develop what many refer to as "all-around fitness," which can require tremendously high levels of training.

In the main, power, speed, agility, balance, flexibility, cardiorespiratory endurance, muscle strength and endurance, neuromuscular coordination, and reaction time are essential ingredients in determining success or failure in a sport. Each individual sport, however, is unique in the level of demands for each of these components. For those interested in participating in multiple sports, it is important to think about the demands of each sport, and the ways that they may help or hinder performance.

In some sports, individual skill-related components play a greater role in determining performance levels. For example, golf and tennis both require power and neuromuscular coordination; however, golf requires excellent balance whereas in tennis, agility and reaction time are most important for successful performance. In some cases, strength in one skill-related component can compensate for deficiency in another. For instance, good coordination and the ability to react quickly may compensate for low levels of muscular strength and power.

If you have become conditioned to a sport that requires a high level of aerobic endurance and then stop training, most of the fitness benefits will be lost within a few months. Resting heart rate, maximal oxygen uptake, and heart rate recovery will all eventually revert back to pre-training levels. The fact that aerobic fitness can be lost so quickly illustrates the need for regular exercise. This is especially so if the aerobic sport is followed by a sport not requiring aerobic endurance. For example, an athlete who participates in demanding aerobic activities such as marathon running or cross-country skiing and then later in the year competes in an anaerobic sport such as tennis or volleyball must include regular aerobic training along with training for the anaerobic sport or face the consequences of losing the aerobic capacity. As with aerobic endurance, gains in strength and anaerobic ability appear to diminish after approximately two months of inactivity.

Before setting up a multisport training program, think about the demands placed on you by each sport. One approach for multiple sports might be to divide your time equally between the sports by following the training requirements for each. Another approach would be to determine your strength or weaknesses for each sport and concentrate your effort on those areas that need work, in addition to maintaining your current level of aerobic or anaerobic fitness and skill performance. For example, an athlete participating in both swimming and tennis might want to build leg strength for additional kicking force and also increase arm strength for a more powerful serve. A three-day-a-week program could be set up using plyometrics (double-leg hops and box jumping) plus Versa Climber workouts for building leg strength and weight resistance cords, free weights, and plyometrics (medicine ball throws) for arm strength.

One should be cautioned that some sports, because of their unique demands, require more practice time than others. A golfer or tennis player might spend two or three continuous hours practicing a skill. On the other hand, because of the physically stressful nature of the sport, a sprint swimmer's practice time is much more limited. In addition, over-concentrating on weaker skills may lead to neglect and deterioration of other skills.

MULTISPORT COMPATIBILITY MATRIX

The multisport matrix on page 228 offers some guidance in determining compatibility between various sports. Essentially, the matrix looks at sports that in themselves might provide some valuable cross-training benefit. For example, a football lineman or linebacker may want to participate in wrestling, where increased opportunities for the development of muscular strength and grappling skills will lead to increased football performance. In other instances, a cross-training sport may be used to maintain or reinforce a level of fitness. An example would be a cross-country skier who runs long distances to ensure high levels of aerobic fitness.

The cross-training sports recommended in the matrix may in some cases complement and in other cases extend or reinforce elements of the sport. To use the matrix, first find your primary sport on one side of the matrix and a second sport on the other. By reading down and across, locate the numbers in the box that correspond to the benefits explained in the key. Remember to keep in mind your strength and weaknesses in your primary sport and factor this into your choice of cross-training sports.

Sport Compatibility Matrix Key

Numbers on the matrix indicate type of benefit derived from multisport participation

1. Enhances or maintains primary-sport energy systems
2. Enhances or maintains all-around general fitness
3. Enhances compatible muscle systems
4. Improves muscle coordination, agility, and skill levels
5. Helps avoid staleness
6. Useful when participation in primary sport is not possible
7. Provides training extension

SPORT COMPATIBILITY MATRIX

SPORTS	Football	Basketball	Baseball	Soccer	Tennis	Alpine Skiing	Golf	Ice Hockey	Wrestling	Track and Field	Nordic Skiing	Distance Running
Football			4,5						1,2,4,7	1,2,3,7		
Basketball				1,2,4,7	2,4					1,2,7		1,2,3,7
Baseball		2,4			2,3,7					2,7		
Soccer		1,2,3,4			3,4						1,3,7	1,3,7
Tennis		2,4,5						1,4		1,7		1,3,7
Alpine Skiing												
Golf												2
Ice Hockey					2,3,4,5							1,3,6,7
Wrestling	1,2,4											1,7
Track and Field	3			1,2,3,7	2,4,5						1,7	
Nordic Skiing				1,2,5,6								1,3,6,7
Distance Running		2,5		1,3,5	2,5		2				1,3,7	
Distance Swimming							2,3,5				1,7	
Distance Cycling							2				1,3,6,7	1,3,6,7
Sprint Running					1,3,5							
Sprint Swimming											1,3,7	
Sprint Cycling					2,5	1,3					1,3,7	
Kayaking/Rowing					2,3,5		2,3				1,6,7	
Speed/In-Line Skating				1,2,3						1,5,7		
Gymnastics												2
Martial Arts									1,4,5			
Racquet- and Handball				1,4,5,7	1,3,4		2,3				1,3,7	1,3,7
Volleyball		2,3,4,5		2,4,5,7	2,4,5	2,4,5						1,7
Cross-Country Skiing		2,5	5	1,2	2,5						1,3,6,7	1,3,7

Distance Swimming	Distance Cycling	Sprint Running	Sprint Swimming	Sprint Cycling	Kayaking/Rowing	Speed/In-Line Skating	Gymnastics	Martial Arts	Racquet- and Handball	Volleyball	Cross-Country Skiing	SPORTS
		1						1,3,4		5		Football
		1,3,7		1,3,7					1,4	3,5	1,2,7	Basketball
		1,3,7		1,2,3,7	1,2,3,7				1,3,4	4,5		Baseball
	1,2,3,7					1,2,5					1,3,7	Soccer
		1,3,7	1,3,7	1,3,7	1,3,7						1,2,7	Tennis
	1,2,6,7			1,3,6,7		2,3,6					1,2,6,7	Alpine Skiing
2,3,5	2				2,3				2,3			Golf
		1,3,6,7		1,3,6,7	1,3,6,7	1,3,4,6						Ice Hockey
	1,5,7	1,7		1,7			1,3		2,4			Wrestling
					1,2,7	2,5						Track and Field
	1,2,3, 5,6,7				1,5,6,7	2,5,6					1,6,7	Nordic Skiing
	1,3,5,7								2,4,5		1,3,7	Distance Running
	1,3,5,7				2,3,7		3					Distance Swimming
				4,7								Distance Cycling
				1,3,7					2,3,5	3,5		Sprint Running
	1,5,6,7				1,3,5,7		3					Sprint Swimming
	1,3,4,7								2,3,7	3,5		Sprint Cycling
				1,6,7		2,4,5,6				4,5,6	1,5,6,7	Kayaking/Rowing
	1,6,7			1,3,6,7							1,7	Speed/In-Line Skating
			1,3,7	1,7					2,3,4,5			Gymnastics
1,3,5,7	1,3,5,7	1,7		1,7					2,4,5		1,7	Martial Arts
1,2,5	1,5,7	1,3,7		1,3,7	1,2,3,7	2,4,5					1,7	Racquet- and Handball
	1,6,7	1,7		1,6,7	1,5,7	2,4,5					1,7	Volleyball
1,5,7	1,5,7		1,3,4,7			2,5			2,3,5			Cross-Country Skiing

*Numbers indicate type of benefit derived from multisport participation.

SPECIAL CONCERNS FOR YOUNG MULTISPORT ATHLETES

Coaches and exercise science specialists are often questioned as to how soon and in what kind of sports a child should start training and participating. More specifically, questions are asked regarding the type, intensity, and duration of the physical training program required for the sports.

Today it is quite common to find young girls in their early teens breaking world records in swimming and gymnastics. Young girls can develop maximum aerobic endurance and muscle strength and are ready to meet the demands of the sport by age 13 or 14. Young boys, on the other hand, will not develop maximum aerobic endurance and muscle strength until their late teens. Children initially should be introduced to gross motor skills involving large-muscle groups such as running, swimming, climbing, cycling, and jumping. Expectations for fine motor or highly skilled movements should be limited until children are psychologically and physically ready.

Early introduction to gross motor activities will allow children to condition the large-muscle groups and prepare their bodies for the transfer to more stressful training later on. Introducing 5-year-olds to 10K races or 12-year-olds to marathon runs is inappropriate both physically and psychologically. On the other hand, a game like soccer would be more appropriate as this activity closely approximates the child's developing physiological and psychological makeup. It is interesting to note that many of the world's top distance runners played soccer as children. Introducing a child to a sport that demands muscle strength and high levels of coordination before they have matured physically can result in frustration and withdrawal from sports participation altogether.

About the Authors

Gary Moran is a research, medical, and forensic biomechanist at Davies Medical Center in San Francisco, and he is the president of Biosports, Inc. He has been a coach, lecturer, and researcher in the areas of running, strength training, and cross-training for more than 30 years. Not only has he worked with athletes at the high school, college, postgraduate, and professional levels, but he has competed on all levels in running, triathlons, weightlifting, and martial arts. He is also a former member of the U.S. Military Pentathlon Team.

Moran received an MA in exercise physiology from San Diego State University in 1971 and a PhD in anatomy and kinesiology from the University of Oregon in 1975. In addition to writing numerous scientific papers on sports medicine and exercise science, he is the coauthor of *Getting Stronger* and *Dynamics of Strength Training*, highly acclaimed books on weight training and physical fitness. A fellow of the American College of Sports Medicine, Dr. Moran has served as director of research at the Nike Shoe Company, associate director of biomechanics at Shriners Hospital for Crippled Children, visiting professor at the University of California, Berkeley, and professor of biomechanics at the University of San Francisco.

Dr. Moran lives in Alameda, California, where he continues to compete in running, triathlons, and martial arts. His other interests include reading and traveling.

George H. McGlynn is a professor and chair of the Exercise and Sports Science Department at the University of San Francisco (USF). In addition, he is director of the USF Human Performance Laboratory and played a key role in establishing the school's graduate program in sports management and fitness. An exercise physiology professor since 1959, McGlynn has written extensively on the subjects of cardiorespiratory fitness and strength training. He is the author of numerous professional articles and five books, including *Dynamics of Fitness* (Fifth Edition), which is one of the most popular fitness texts on the market. He also has worked as a fitness consultant for many college and professional athletic teams and for state and local government agencies.

McGlynn received an EdD from the University of California, Berkeley, in 1966. He was presented the Distinguished Teaching and Research Award by the University of San Francisco in 1989 and became a member of the New York State Athletic Hall of Fame in 1987. A resident of San Francisco, California, McGlynn's leisure activities including skiing, cycling, and oil painting.

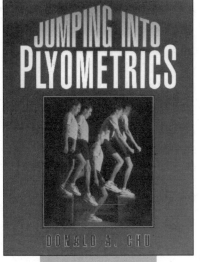